HOUSES NOW:
UNIQUE HOUSES

Edition 2007

Author: Eduard Broto
Editorial Coordinator: Jacobo Krauel
Graphic designer & production: Oriol Vallès
Text: Contributed by the architects, edited by William George and Marta Rojals

© Carles Broto i Comerma
Jonqueres, 10, 1-5
08003 Barcelona, Spain
Tel.: +34 93 301 21 99
Fax: +34-93-301 00 21
E-mail: info@linksbooks.net
www.linksbooks.net

HOUSES NOW:
UNIQUE HOUSES

index

introduction

"There's no place like home," goes the adage, to which we might add "especially if yours is one of the houses shown on the following pages." Indeed, there is nothing standardized about these highly unconventional dwellings, which have been designed strictly for (and by) the adventurer at heart.

They are "experimental" in the sense that there were no existing prototypes to work from and that, in many cases, the designs break all the commonly-accepted rules of house architecture. In some cases, it was nothing more than a concept that formed the basis of the program (such is the case with the home patterned after the Möbius strip or the scheme based on Salvador Dali's statements on the future of architecture); in others, the lifestyles of the clients themselves were the source of inspiration behind a personalized scheme - one house designed specifically for musicians takes on the shape of the inner ear!

The only trait the following projects have in common is that each radically defies convention in its own unique way.

To provide further depth and cohesion, we have also included an array of explanatory information and floor plans provided by the architects themselves.

Arturo Frediani

Garriga Poch House

Photographs: Eugeni Pons,
Ramón Prat, Arturo Frediani

Lles de Cerdanya,
Spain

For this single-family house in the mountains, the designers wanted to keep the architectural dialogue as far removed as possible from the issues that so obsessed the authors of local building laws. Instead, they sought their own freedom of movement within the allowable margins.

While viewing the more specific paragraphs governing material use with reticence, the architects had no objection to the extensive application of those already used throughout the town: wood, Arabian tile and stone. The only condition that they imposed was that materials should be subject to direct use at all times (as opposed to a merely token cover-up), whether via technological or traditional methods.

The only two original walls that were still standing were worked into the new program. Their 28 inches (70 cm) of thickness, stone structure and load-bearing capabilities were used as the pattern on which the new walls would be built. The steel structure and wooden framework of the facades was inspired on the construction principles of a Steinway & Sons grand piano. The metal structure was introduced in order to ensure the dimensional stability of the wooden elements as the building ages.

The floor plan, in the shape of an eight, is split into two distinct sections joined by a 6½ -foot-wide (2 m) neck. The main section is a fully-equipped apartment with the master bedroom. The other can be used as an independent dwelling with the installation of kitchen fittings. When separated, the stairwells of each section enable independent access to the top floor.

The clients requested the maximum fluidity between the interior of the ground floor and the garden. Although openings in traditional houses in this region are generally quite small, only rarely exceeding 4 feet (1.2 meters) in width, the laws concerning windows do not limit their size along the south-facing facades. Fortunately, it was not specified anywhere how they should open; it was thus assumed that the enclosure could be a shutter-like element.

Such sizing, as well as the proportions of the other ground floor windows, presented considerable challenges in carrying out the project according to a traditional system. The demands of the client thereby depended on the applicability of a system capable of manually moving shutters of up to 75 sq ft (7 sq m) and weighing some 288 lbs (130 kg) with ease.

After working on a system using the fittings of the sliding door of a van, and subsequently abandoning the idea (they thought the bearings might eventually stick with ice), the architects used the doors on the luggage compartments of a bus as the basis for a new system. However, in contrast to their source of inspiration, their design is free of guide tracks and features two pendulum-like arms instead of just one. The shutters are thus supported at two points and balanced by a third. A prototype measuring 14 square inches (35 sq cm) in surface area with 16-inch-long (40 cm) arms was perfected in the workshop. Having achieved satisfactory results, a life-sized model that multiplied the size by 20 and the arm by 4 was put to the test.

Site plan

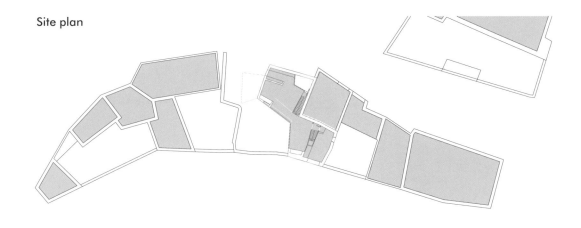

The floor plan, in the shape of an eight, is split into two distinct sections joined by a 6½ -foot-wide (2 m) neck. The main section is a fully-equipped apartment with the master bedroom. The other can be used as an independent dwelling with the installation of kitchen fittings. When separated, the stairwells of each section enable independent access to the top floor.

© Arturo Frediani

Ground floor plan
1. Yard
2. Living room
3. Garage
4. Dining room
5. Chimney room

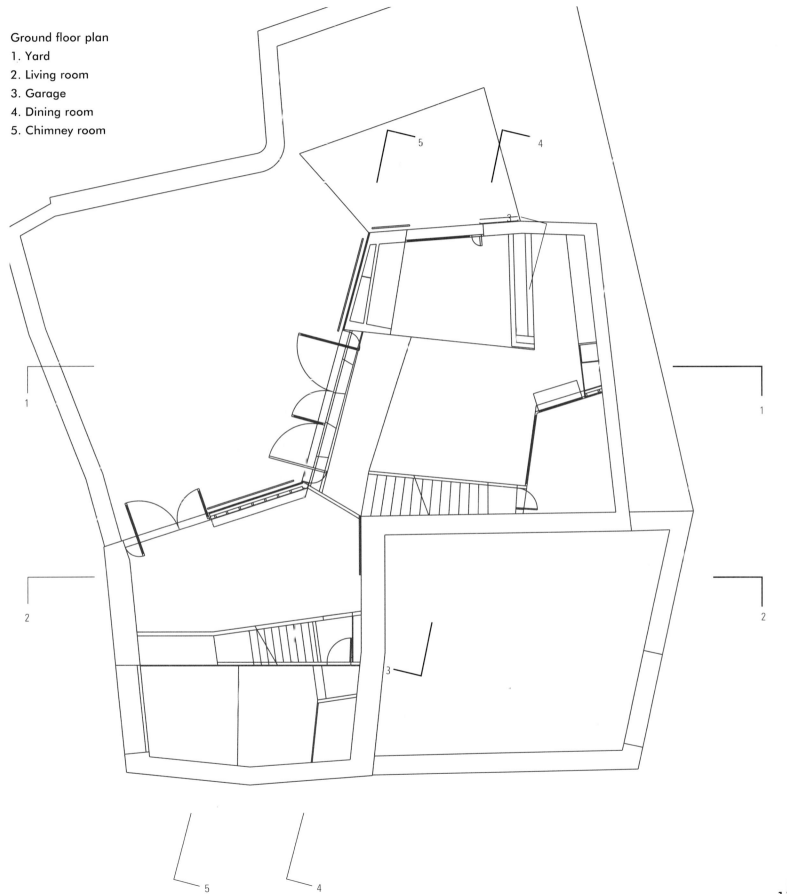

First floor plan

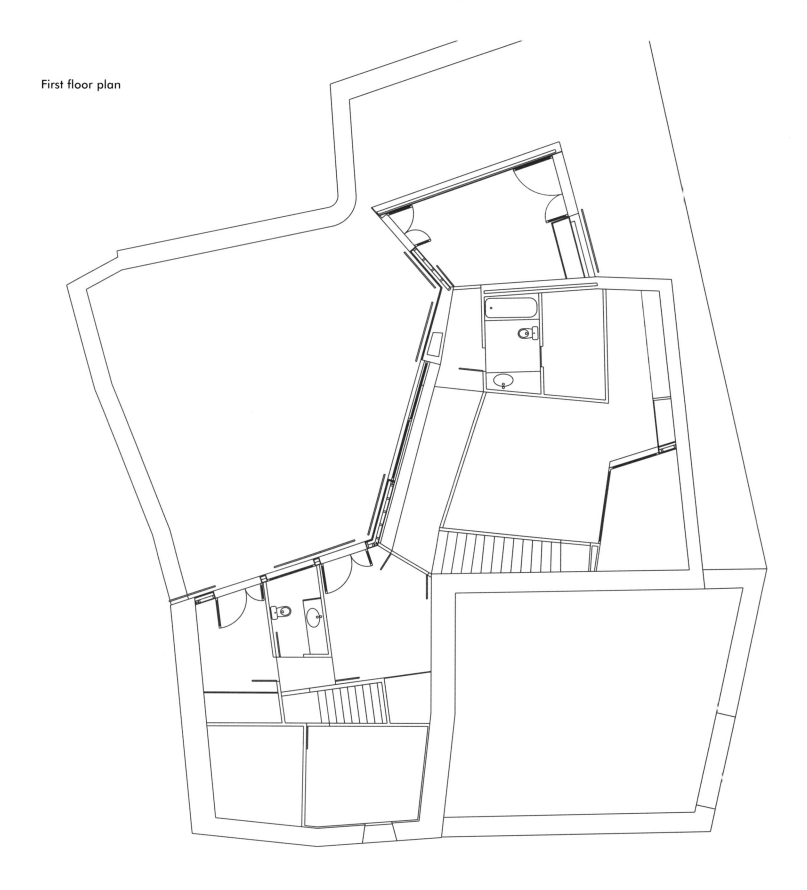

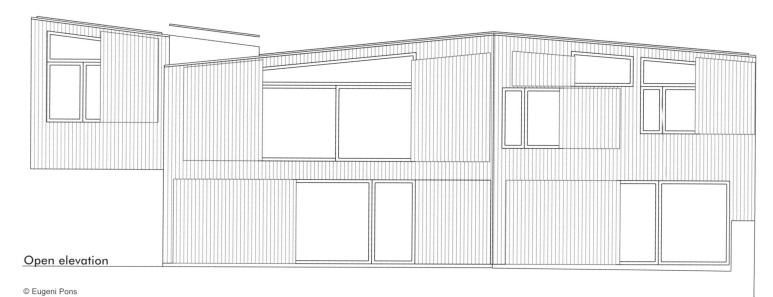

Open elevation

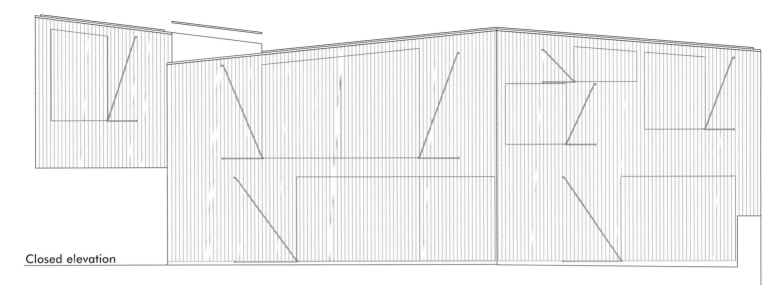

Closed elevation

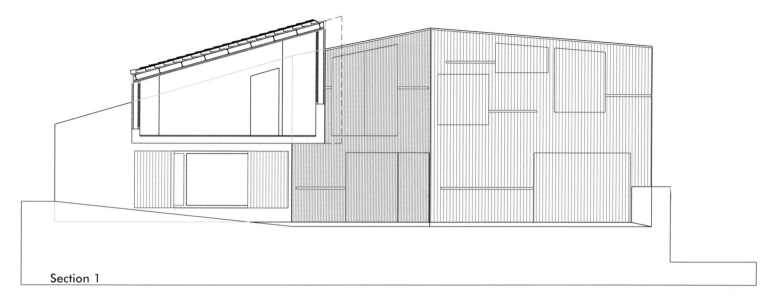

Section 1

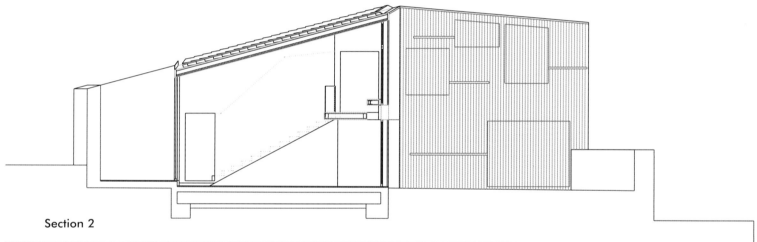

Section 2

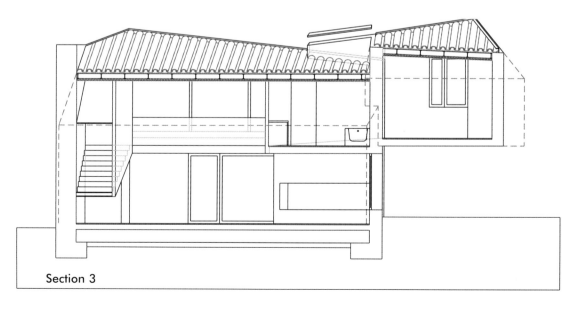

Section 3

The shutters are thus supported at two points and balanced by a third. A prototype measuring 14 square inches (35 sq cm) in surface area with 16-inch-long (40 cm) arms was perfected in the workshop. Having achieved satisfactory results, a life-sized model that multiplied the size by 20 and the arm by 4 was put to the test.

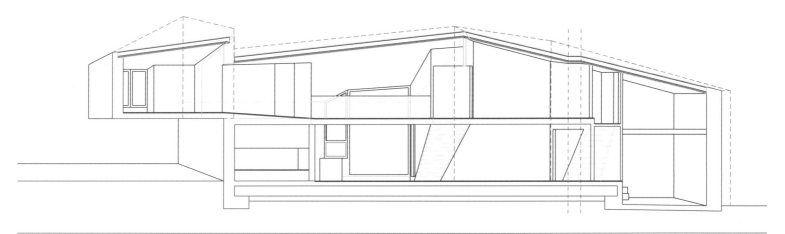

© Eugeni Pons

Section 5

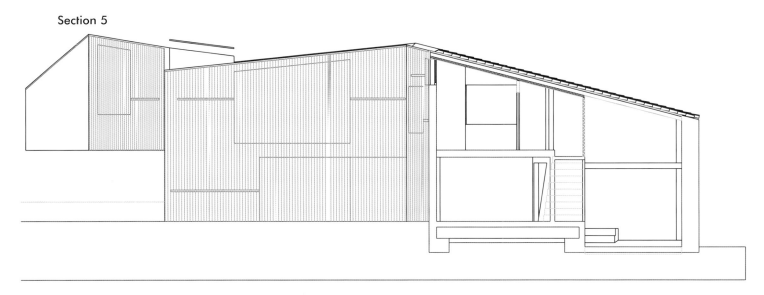

© Eugeni Pons

Construction detail

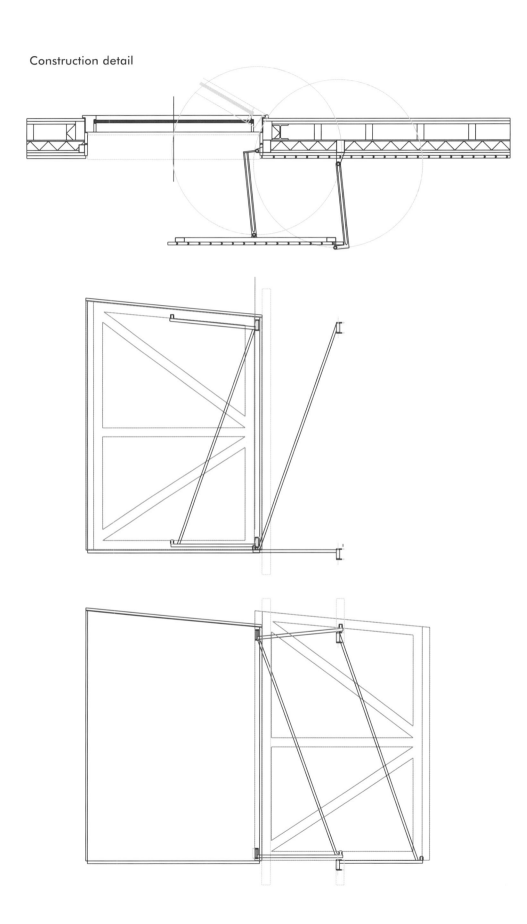

Carlos Zapata,
Wood + Zapata

Private House

Photographs: Undine Pröhl

Quito, Ecuador

Located on a spectacular site minutes outside of Quito, this private house has just been completed. The 8000-square-foot main house features four bedrooms, six bathrooms, kitchen, dining room, living room, playroom, family room and an artist's studio adjacent to the master bedroom.

A profusion of unexpected geometries greets the inhabitants at every turn - there is scarcely a right angle in the entire design, with entirely glazed walls tilting outward, angled doorways and gentle curves coming together in one unified whole. The warmth of wood contrasts with the home's extensive glazed surfaces.

One of the most unusual features of the house is the lap pool that begins inside the house and continues outside to cantilever over the cliff. The walkway alongside the pool cantilevers out even further, offering a sweeping view of the Andes Mountains sitting opposite the site.

The structure of the building is primarily of reinforced concrete and has been designed to withstand earthquakes.

Much of the artwork showcased in the house is the work of the owner's father, Oswaldo Viteri, who is one of the most recognized artists in Ecuador.

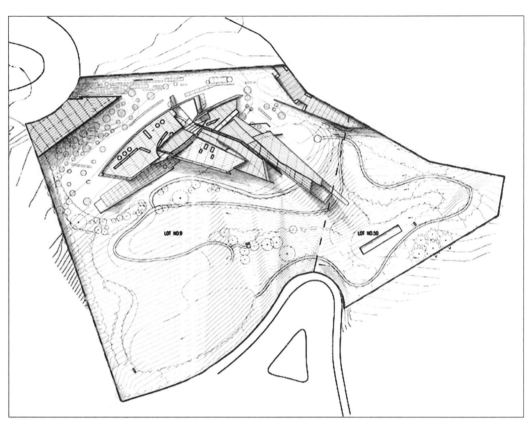

The curved wall of the east faced has been designed to isolate the home from its built surroundings. There, the anti-seismic reinforced concrete structure has been left unfinished on the lower level and clad in metal on the upper part to camouflage the only two windows.

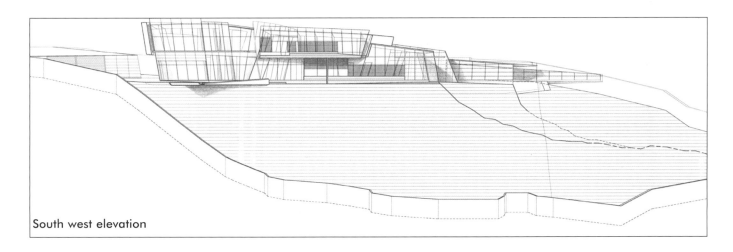

South west elevation

The layout of the house is almost traditional, with public functions and a separate service area on the ground floor and the private area upstairs. The main stairs feature a curved surface that is reflected on the first floor in the volume of the master bedroom.

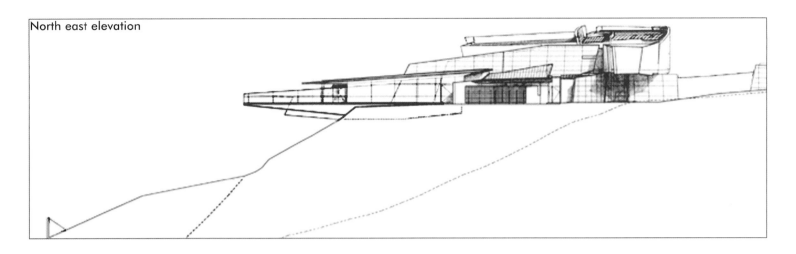
North east elevation

Harry Seidler & Associates

House in the Southern Highlands

Photographs: Eric Sierins /
Max Dupain & Associates

**New South Wales,
Australia**

The site for this house is the crest of a rugged escarpment, overlooking a winding river far below and surrounded by a vast area of wilderness.

The house is placed against a large rock platform, with a suspended living area and projecting balcony overlooking the dramatic natural setting.

Following the rock plateau, the plan is arranged on two levels, with the glazed pavilion of the living area positioned below the more enclosed bedroom wing. The floor structure is of concrete and the sweepingly profiled roofs of the living pavilion, bedroom wing and garage are framed with curved steel beams. These profiles, which are composed from a series of differing radii, are possible due to new technologies in the steel industry.

The projecting balcony jutting out over the cliff edge is hung from the roof's steel columns, with diagonal braces. Like the offset curved roofs, these structural members create a gravity-defying dramatic effect.

In contrast to the suspended roof structure, the house is anchored into the rugged terrain by projecting random rubble stone screen walls, support piers and retaining walls, all built from the ample sandstone boulders collected from the site. The continuous sandstone retaining wall creates a tie between garage, house and the swimming pool, which is positioned and retained between two large rock outcrops to the north of the house. In bushfire mode, the pool water is pumped to sprinklers hidden under the eaves and projecting living areas. The house is built entirely of fireproof materials, reinforced concrete floors, white block and stone walls with a steel roof structure.

Due to lack of access to town water and sewerage, rainwater is collected from the roofs and stored in a very large central storage tank under the house. Waste water is chemically treated and used for irrigation.

To be largely energy sufficient, stone fireplaces are used throughout the house. They also act as dividing elements, defining specific areas within the mostly open-planned space.

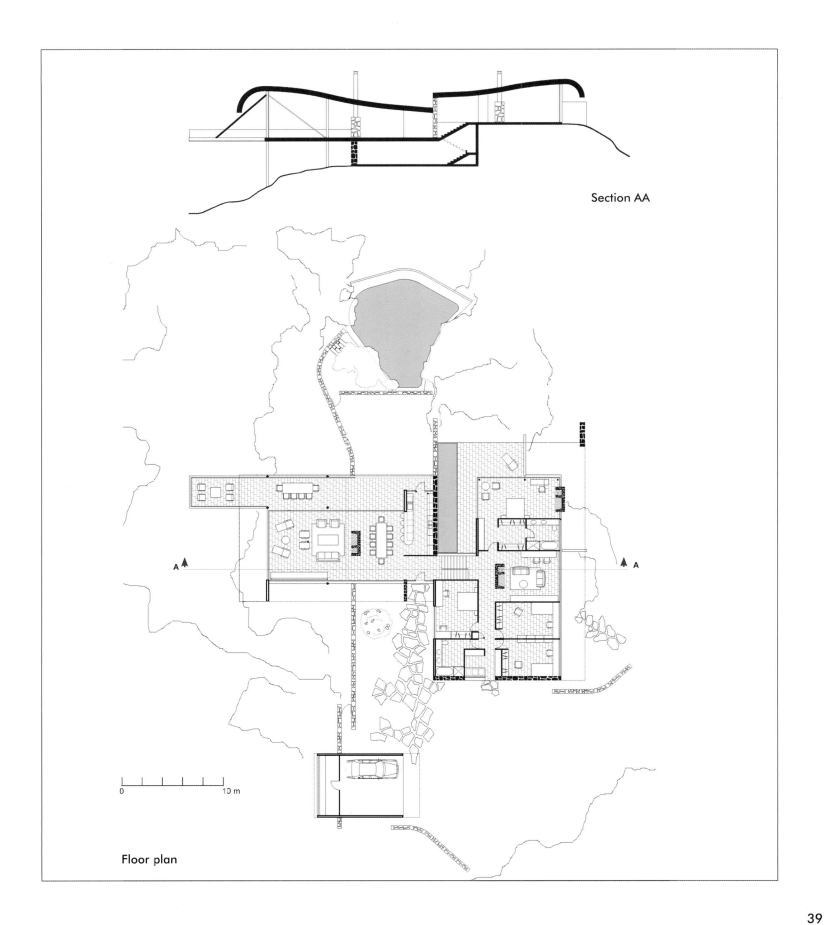

Section AA

Floor plan

0   10 m

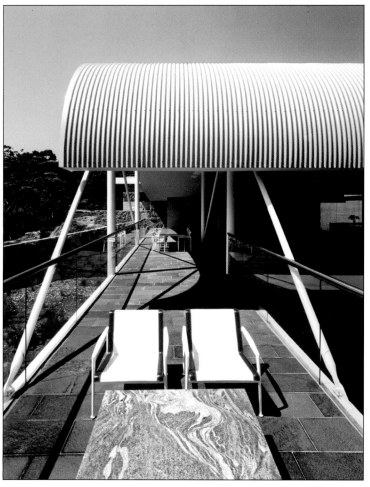

Living space is spacious, with breathtaking views.
A suspended steel balcony enhances the drama.

hobby a., Wolfgang Maul & Walter Schuster

House for Eva and Fritz

*Photographs:
Fritz Hauswirth, hobby.a*

**Bergheim/Salzburg
, Austria**

Being a young self-employed photographer and an advertising agent the owners asked for a home that reflects the flexible, mobile and temporary character of their profession and that, nevertheless, fits into the surroundings and is more charming than an ordinary, soulless trailer.

The architects' primary objective was a monolithic block with a homogeneous exterior design that corresponds with the industrial context in the neighbourhood. As first experiments with a coating of polyurethane or fibreglass respectively failed, a prestressed membrane structure from PVC coated polyester highdensity yarn was found the ideal material. Just imagine a house in Emma Peel's appealing gear.

This smooth skin covers a light construction of twelve pieces of insulated woodwork that were prefabricated at the carpenter's and assembled at the site. The wooden elements consist of orientated span boards (OSB) both inside and outside which are mounted onto the supporting wooden stays with insulation in-between. Allowing three centimetres of airing, the synthetic membrane is stretched smoothly over the rounded edges of the building. Only then the window-outlets are cut with Stanley-knives and the edges of the membrane pulled in again. This processing does not need any kind of metal sheets, which results in a homogeneous body. The semi-permeable membrane shows the same characteristics as the well-known material Gore-Tex, humidity is transported to the outside but not the other way round.

A different story is the rounded edges and corners of the house: ever so simple as effective. A quarter-segment of a polocal tube with a diameter of 50 centimetres each forms an elevation. The corners take up 14 elements of exact sphere segments altogether, which were moulded for that very purpose.

The aesthetics of these unusual materials flash light onto an architectural taboo. Synthetic materials surround us, whether in shops, cars or our workplaces. Only architecture pretends that there have not been any new materials since Vitruvius. Embarrassed, we conceal the entire choice of contemporary materials, such as Styrofoam insulation, PU-foam or silicon-synthetic resin, behind plastering, natural-stone facades and wooden grating.

Emanating from some Austrian regions, an ideology has won recognition that propagates the restoration of genuine wood-constructions, which actually consist of epoxy-soaked wood-shavings. This house is a thorn in the side of the theory of regionalism as a confinement to form and/or material. Should regionalism be of any relevance in a global context, it is to be reconsidered thoroughly and without the least fear. Otherwise it might fall back on a new provincialism sooner or later.

46

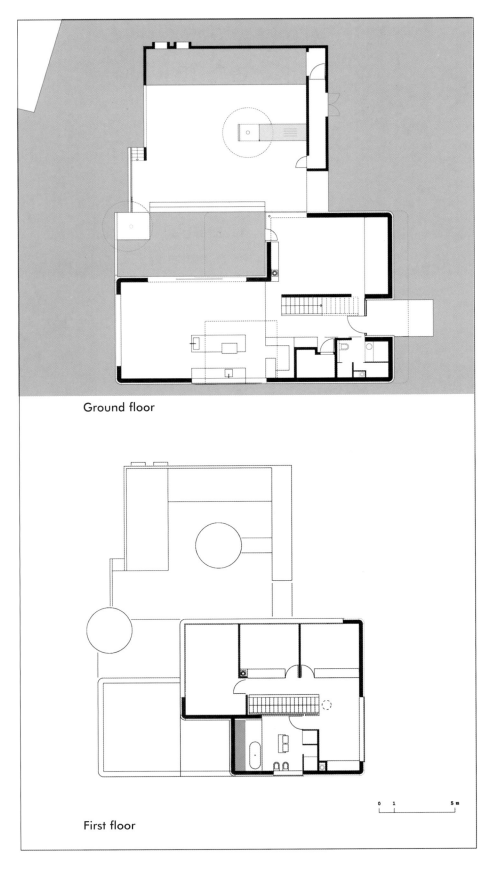

Ground floor

First floor

0 1   5 m

The architects' primary objective was a mono-lithic block with a homogeneous exterior design that corresponds with the industrial context in the neighbourhood. A prestressed membrane structure from PVC coated polyester highdensity yarn was found the ideal material.

South elevation

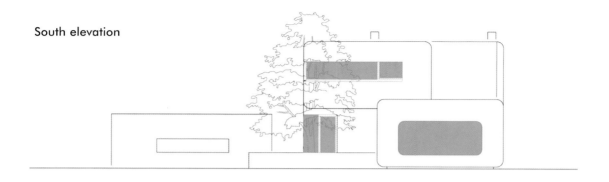

Section

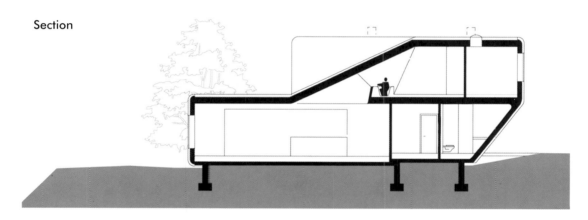

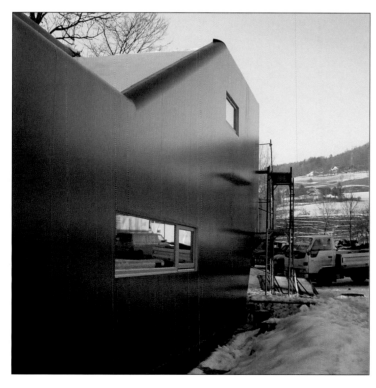

50

Jun Aoki

House I

*Photographs:
Tsunejiro Watanabe*

Tokyo, Japan

The most has been made of this relatively small plot. Of the 61 sqm of available ground space, a two-story home with a basement has been built on just 37 sqm (the total floor area is 109 sqm). However, its impact on the surrounding neighborhood cannot be judged by its size alone. The eye-catching and unexpected geometry of the facade sets this home apart from the rest.

The project is a sculpted concrete shell placed in the space between two existing houses. Broadly speaking, the structure is comprised of two independent volumes placed within the shell. The upper floor, from which is seemingly suspended a glass-enclosed mezzanine overlooking the dining room, comprise the first volume; the second is made up of the ground floor, which encloses the basement space.

The primary structural system is of reinforced concrete. The facades are clad in wood paneling, with windows framed in aluminum and steel.

In the interior, the sleek, modern look of steel and concrete competes with the homey warmth of wood. High and wide expanses of exposed concrete slabs make an imposing wall cladding. The floors are done almost entirely in unstained wood throughout the home, the only exception being the unique flooring material used in the mezzanine: leather.

Painted steel stairways and handrails, and custom-designed steel cabinets are the elements which provide the necessary dark visual counterweight to the light tones of concrete and unstained wood.

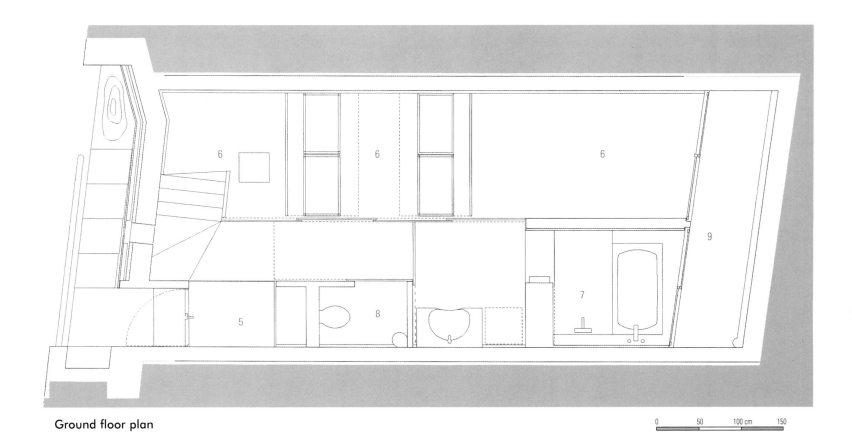

Ground floor plan

0   50   100 cm   150

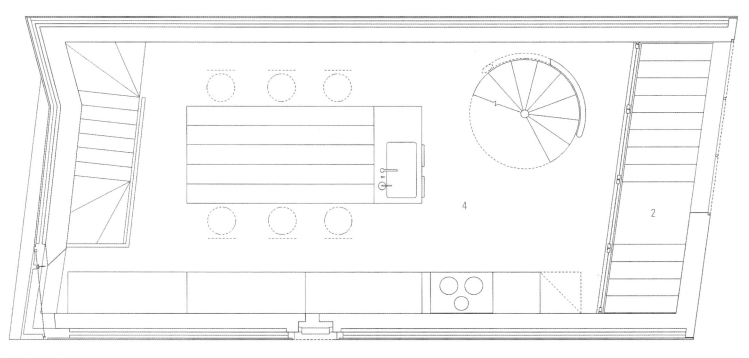

First floor plan

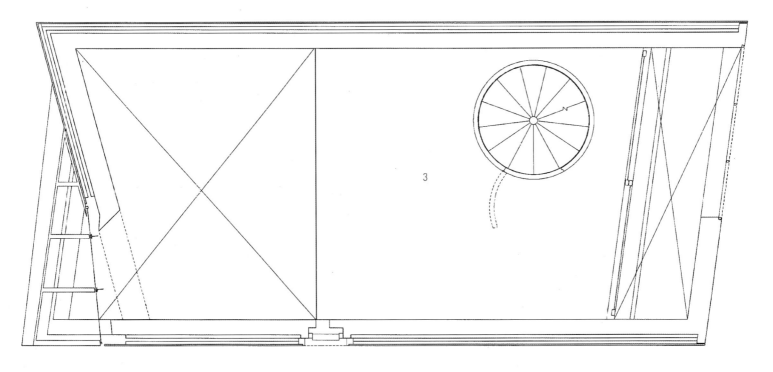

Mezzanine

1. Study
2. Terrace
3. Bedroom

4. Kitchen
5. Entrance
6. Storage

7. Bathroom
8. WC
9. Areaway

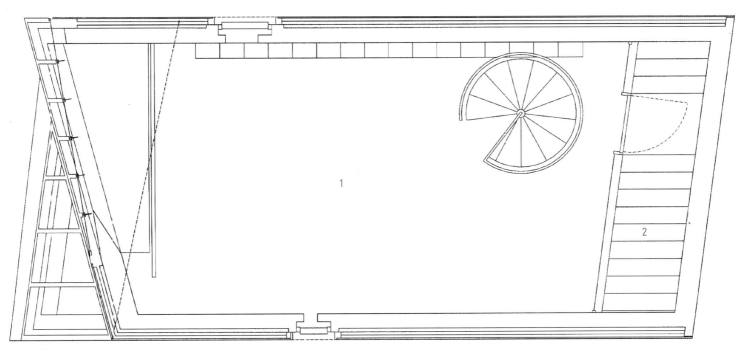

Second floor plan

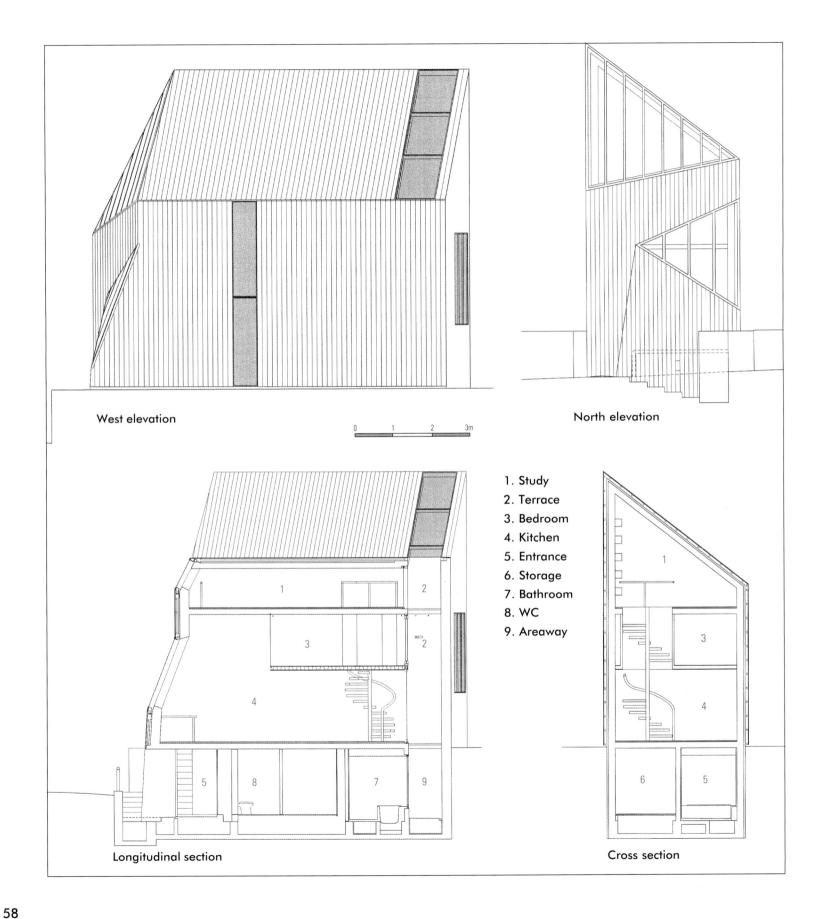

West elevation

North elevation

0   1   2   3m

1. Study
2. Terrace
3. Bedroom
4. Kitchen
5. Entrance
6. Storage
7. Bathroom
8. WC
9. Areaway

Longitudinal section

Cross section

The walls are clad in high and wide expanses of exposed concrete. The floors are done almost entirely in unstained wood, the only exception being the unique flooring material used in the mezzanine: leather.

Jyrki Tasa

Moby Dick House

Photographs: Jyrki Tasa, Jussi Tianen

Espoo, Finland

This biomorphic house designed for a family of four is perched on a base of massive natural rocks. A stairway built from stone and a steel bridge lead to the main entrance on the first floor above ground level. One enters the building, which has a surface area of approximately 6135 sq ft (570 sq m) through an organically-shaped, stark white outer wall. On this floor there is a living-room (with a steel fireplace clad in brushed aluminum plates), a library, master bedroom and two balconies. The ground floor houses the children's spaces, a guestroom and a garage. The basement contains sauna facilities, a fireplace and a gym.

The various spaces are alternately connected via three translucent bridges made of glass and steel. Changes in level are joined by an impressive double-height winter garden and a tall spiraling staircase, which features a steel shell with oak steps and a tubular steel handrail with steel wires. This staircase, which forms the spatial core of the house, is lit by a large skylight. From the staircase one has a view in all directions of the house - either directly or through diverse glass walls.

The organically-shaped ceiling on the first floor complements the free-form spatial organization suggested by the curved white outer wall. All interior walls are rectangular in section, as opposed to the outer shell, which forms a dynamic contrast between the two. Large windows expose the house to views toward the southwest and the garden in order to capture the best light in the winter. The house's energy system is complemented by underfloor heating. The structural framework of the house consists of concrete-filled steel pillars and composite slabs of concrete and steel combined with a roof construction in steel and wood. The facades are mostly clad in plywood, along with pine slats and boards. The undulating first-floor ceiling consists of overlapping birch veneer plates, making it possible to cover the organic form bending in two directions.

The various spaces are alternately connected via three translucent bridges made of glass and steel. Changes in level are joined by an impressive double-height winter garden and a tall spiraling staircase, which features a steel shell with oak steps and a tubular steel handrail with steel wires. This staircase, which forms the spatial core of the house, is lit by a large skylight.

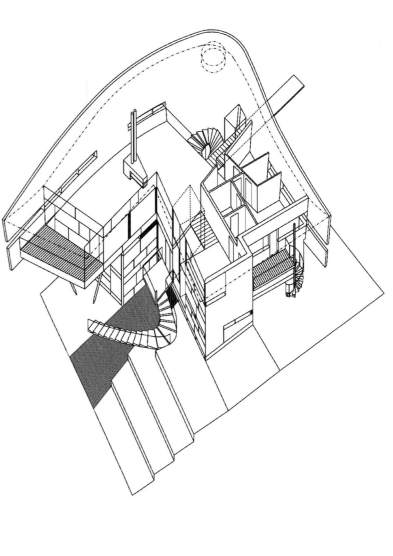

Site plan

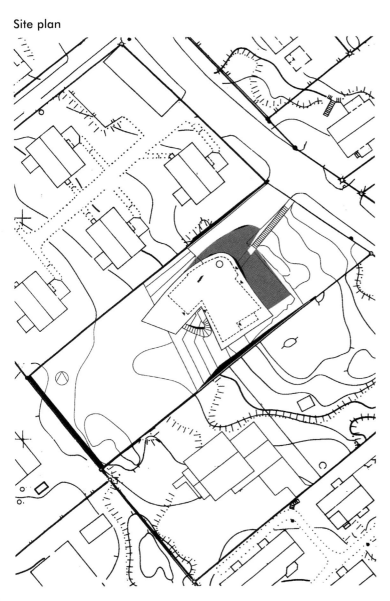

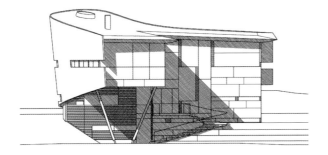

South west elevation

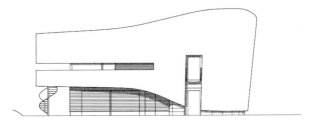

North east elevation

© Jussi Tianen

© Jussi Tianen

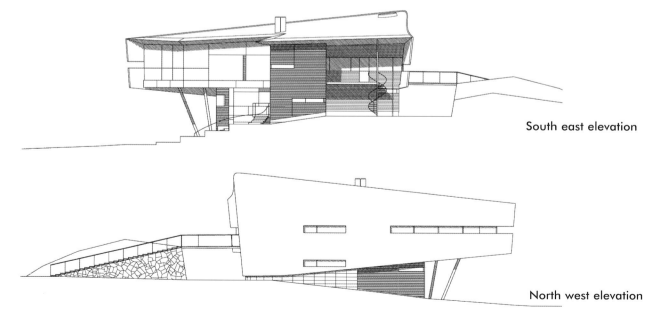

South east elevation

North west elevation

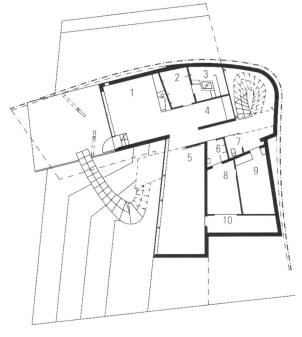

Basement floor plan

1. Sauna cabinet
2. Bathroom
3. Sauna
4. Dressing room
5. Gym
6. Cleaning room
7. Toilet
8. Technical equipment
9. Wine cellar
10. Storage
11. Bedroom
12. Clothes store

13. Bedroom
14. Winter garden
15. Hall
16. Garage
17. Terrace
18. Study
19. Living room
20. Clothes
21. Kitchen
22. Utility room
23. Balcony

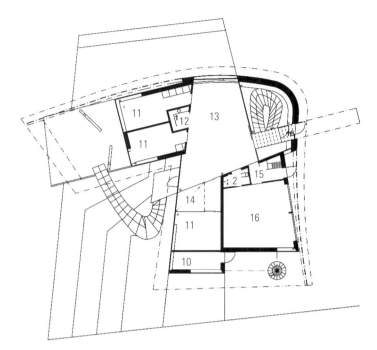

Ground floor plan

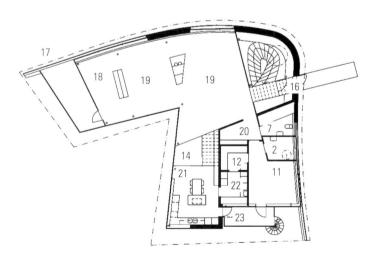

First floor plan

Kohki Hiranuma / Hs Workshop - ASIE

MINNA no IE

Photographs:
Hs Workshop - ASIA

Kusatsu-shi Shiga, Japan

This three-story house has a total floor area of just under 100 sqm and was designed for two households together comprising six people. The average height of the inhabitants is relatively short, around 1.5 meters, which led to the idea of creating a project centered around the small-sized volume on a human scale.

The site is rectangular and measures 11 x 8 meters. The clients' demands, paired with local building regulations, created a "condition" for the architect, the objective of which was developed within a "representation".

The first basic condition projected a matrix of 6.4 sqm. The generational gap is reflected in the shift to the left and right, upward and downward of the floors. In the process of adjusting these conditions, this gap is lessened if the floors shift 0.3 meters in direction XY.

With these requisites, an expressive method is introduced that is also reflected in the horizontal timber frame structure.

All the lines of the structure are distributed in the four directions so that an arc of 10 meters in diameter is inversely repeated along the midsection of the building. Thus, the requirements have been met, and the gaps bridged.

Concept diagram

Process diagram

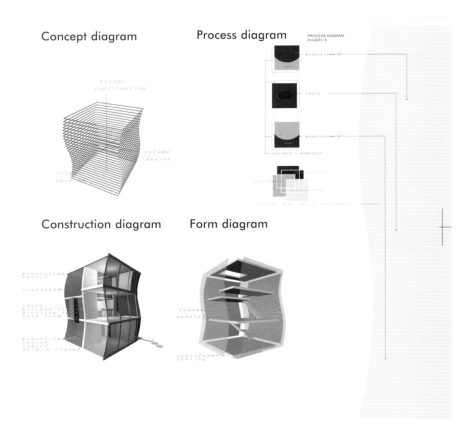

Construction diagram

Form diagram

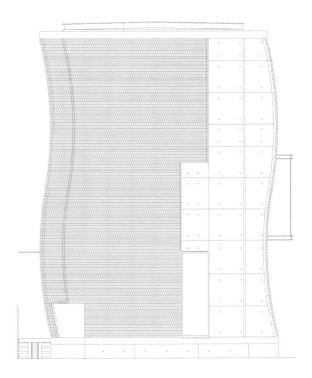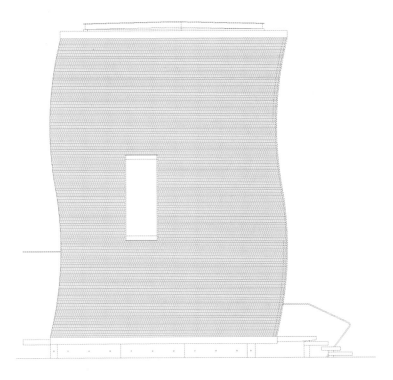

The house is a representation of the generational gap among the inhabitants destined to live in it: the exterior profile, which the architect refers to as "fluctuation-movement", is an allegory of these differences, allowing each individual to feel and speak through movement.

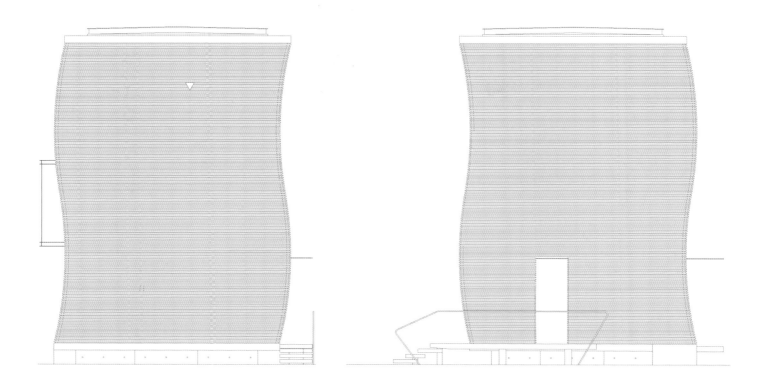

Ground floor plan · First floor plan · Second floor plan · Roof plan

1. Walkway
2. Entrance
3. Courtyard
4. Space 2
5. Space 1
6. Walk-in closet
7. Kitchen
8. Space 3
9. Space 4
10. Terrace
11. Void
12. Roof

Sections

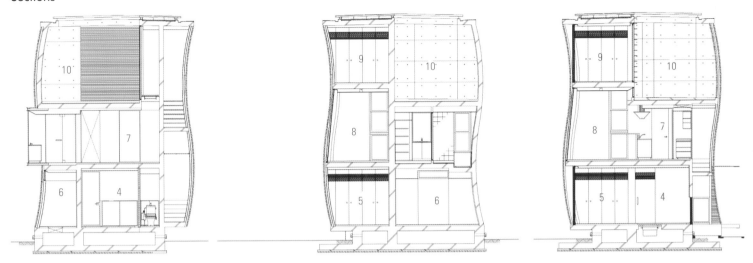

1. Walkway
2. Entrance
3. Courtyard
4. Space 2
5. Space 1
6. Walk-in closet
7. Kitchen
8. Space 3
9. Space 4
10. Terrace
11. Void
12. Roof

In the interior, each floor scarcely reaches 40m^2 of floor area, yet each inhabitant nonetheless enjoys personal space. This was one of the clients' requirements: a "condition" that the architect worked into a "representation" in the project.

Manuel Herz

"Legal / Illegal"

Photographs: Boris Becker

Cologne, Germany

This building is the result of a developer's reluctant decision to use architecture to add value to his investment in a complex historical and regulatory context in the city of Bayenthal. The 5.5 x 25 m site, together with heritage, planning and safety regulations, set the conditions for a very clearly defined and unambiguous volume, a transparent orthogonal building set one meter back from the street. As a full construction covering the whole site was not allowed, the volume is reduced by terraces on each level that step down the rear of the building.

In contrast to this "legal" volume conditioned by regulations, there is a second "defiant" volume, a non-orthogonal, free-formed body that exceeds the maximum permitted floor area. It is mainly opaque and traces a path from street level through the heritage-listed gate, moving up and through the floors, with its main mass at the upper levels facing back down the street. It's windows, goggle-eyed, look into the sky, onto the terraces and down onto the street. Every surface of its faceted volume throws a "shadow area" onto one of the neighboring sites, its irregular shape allowing it to disregard the corresponding regulations and to encroach on the municipal building line on the street. Not a single exterior wall is perpendicular, and the distinctions between wall, floor and ceilings are blurred.

The volume is covered with a red polyutherane coating with allows for a "construction without details" and forms a continuous skin over all surfaces of the building.

By creating a building that combines a volume which respects legal requirements and a second, disrespectful volume, a foreign element is introduced into the urban fabric. The building attempts to enrich its context and express the area's historical and present problems by pushing the limits architecturally.

Site plan

GOLTSTEINSTRAßE

CÄSARSTRAßE

This new building is set on a narrow site measuring 5.5 x 25 meters in the historical district of the city. Its construction was subject to strict norms governing the heritage of the site, norms which the architects adhered to on the lower volume, but violated on the upper.

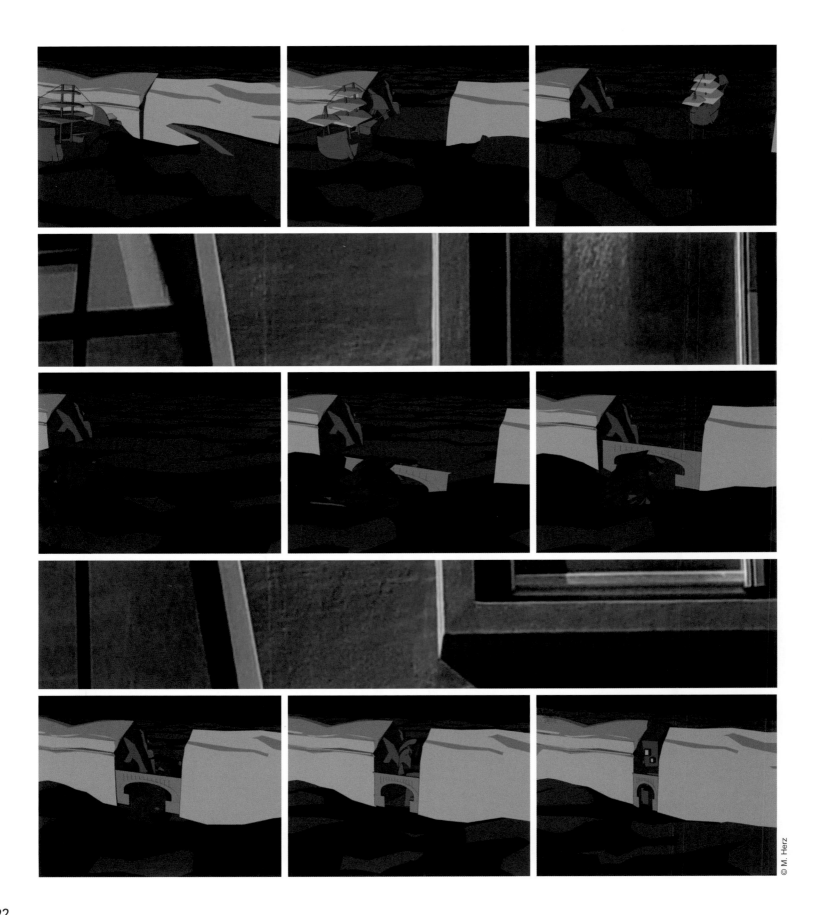

"Legal" part of the building showing codes that have shaped the building

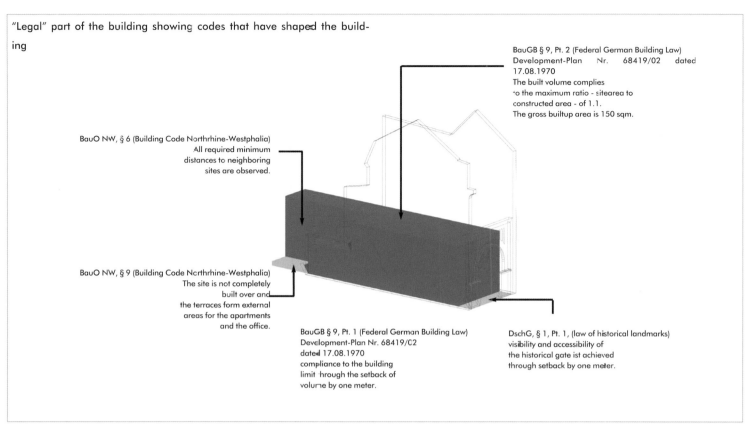

BauO NW, § 6 (Building Code Northrhine-Westphalia)
All required minimum
distances to neighboring
sites are observed.

BauO NW, § 9 (Building Code Northrhine-Westphalia)
The site is not completely
built over and
the terraces form external
areas for the apartments
and the office.

BauGB § 9, Pt. 2 (Federal German Building Law)
Development-Plan Nr. 68419/02 dated
17.08.1970
The built volume complies
to the maximum ratio - sitearea to
constructed area - of 1.1.
The gross builtup area is 150 sqm.

BauGB § 9, Pt. 1 (Federal German Building Law)
Development-Plan Nr. 68419/02
dated 17.08.1970
compliance to the building
limit through the setback of
volume by one meter.

DschG, § 1, Pt. 1, (law of historical landmarks)
visibility and accessibility of
the historical gate ist achieved
through setback by one meter.

"Illegal" part of the building with violated building codes

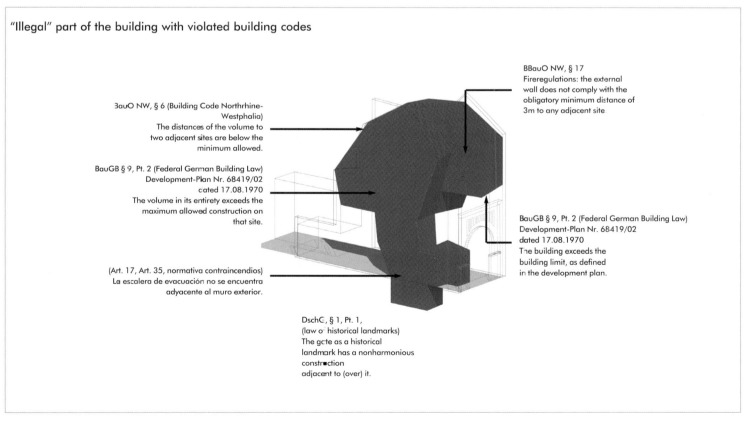

BauO NW, § 6 (Building Code Northrhine-
Westphalia)
The distances of the volume to
two adjacent sites are below the
minimum allowed.

BauGB § 9, Pt. 2 (Federal German Building Law)
Development-Plan Nr. 68419/02
dated 17.08.1970
The volume in its entirety exceeds the
maximum allowed construction on
that site.

(Art. 17, Art. 35, normativa contraincendios)
La escalera de evacuación no se encuentra
adyacente al muro exterior.

BBauO NW, § 17
Fireregulations: the external
wall does not comply with the
obligatory minimum distance of
3m to any adjacent site

BauGB § 9, Pt. 2 (Federal German Building Law)
Development-Plan Nr. 68419/02
dated 17.08.1970
The building exceeds the
building limit, as defined
in the development plan.

DschG, § 1, Pt. 1,
(law of historical landmarks)
The gate as a historical
landmark has a nonharmonious
construction
adjacent to (over) it.

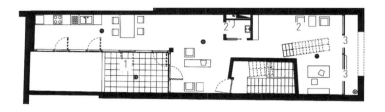

Level -1

1. Filing room (for the office)
2. Cellars
3. Machinery rooms

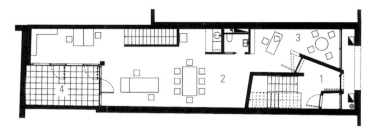

Level 0

1. Common entrance area
2. Office unit
3. Reception / waiting/talking
4. Inner court

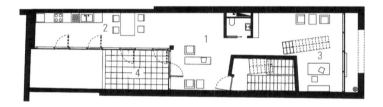

Level 1

Lower apartment:
1. Hall, Living
2. Cooking, eating
3. Living, working
4. Terrace

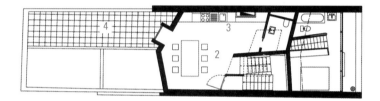

Level 2

Lower apartment:
1. Sleeping
Upper Apartment:
2. Entrance, eating
3. Cooking
4. Terrace

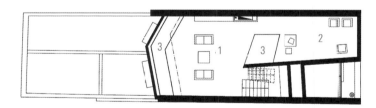

Level 3

Upper apartment:
1. Living, celebrating
2. Reading, watching TV
3. Attics

Level 4

Tal
1. Working
2. Sleeping
3. Attics

Longitudinal sections

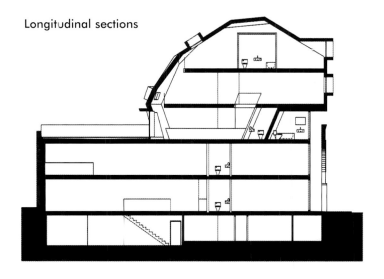

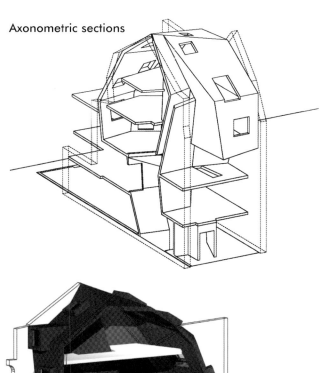
Axonometric sections

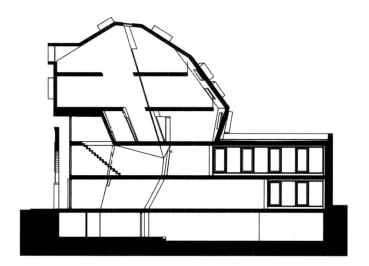

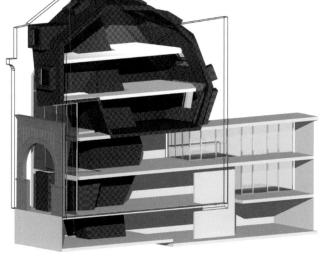

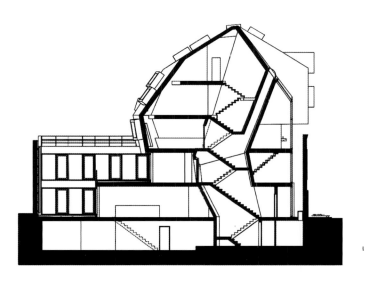

Cross sections

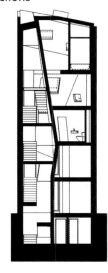

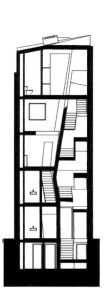

The interior unfolds throughout the five floors in a geometrically anarchistic progression. The only parallel lines shaping the space are those of the structural system, while the walls, voids and railings break up the orthogonality.

Monolab Architects

Body House

Photographs:
MONOLAB Architects

**Rotterdam,
The Netherlands**

The site of this house is situated in one of three rows of seven houses each, in the Katendrecht residential redevelopment on a harbour pier that was previously part of Rotterdam's China Town.

The initial design concept was connecting the kitchen/dining heart of the building to the exterior, which was resolved by developing a wire frame and covering this with a skin to contain service spaces. The building is like a living organism, with its central heart and a faceted eye looking out over the river. The frame is angular, cut like a rough diamond and covered by different types of skins: metal grill, glass and particle sheet with epoxy coating and synthetic fabric.

The Body House is an urban stack of three small projects, with the lower and the upper embodying opposing housing concepts. Below is the fixed, interiorized, dark, heavy base, a cast concrete plinth that is a kind of ground floor basement area. On top is the roof terrace reflecting a campsite with a free, open, light and flexible nylon tent.

In between, a steel cage consisting of a series of columns and beams placed on the plinth defines the living area. The steel structure of the body stabilises the whole building, carrying part of the concrete floor with its foot and connected to the roof beams at the top, and pushing out the big window towards the panoramic river view. Four types of openings physically connect the body to the outside: a pivoting entry slab, a flip door to the patio, a tilting plank to the terrace and a shifting tablet to the roof.

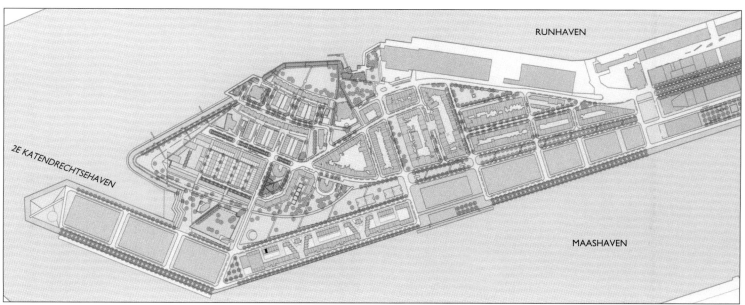

Site plan

The Body House is an urban stack of three small projects: a solid, opaque concrete base below, an open, light roof terrace with a flexible nylon tent above, and the body in the living area in-between.

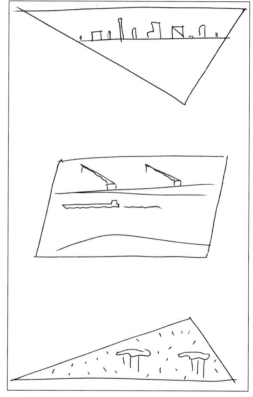

The building is like a living organism, with its central heart and a faceted eye looking out over the river. The body wire frame is angular, cut like a rough diamond, connecting the different parts of the building, from the concrete base to the roof and the large window that is the main feature of the facade.

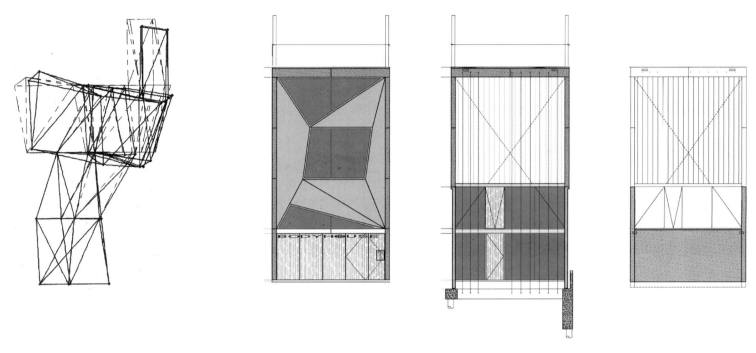

1. Entry
2. Storage
3. Bedroom
4. Bathroom
5. Patio
6. Living
7. Terrace
8. Dining / kitchen
9. Transparent floor
10. Roof terrace

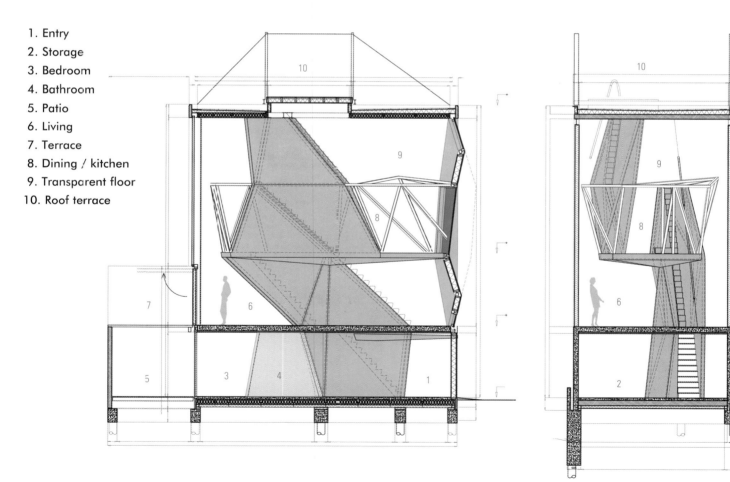

Norisada Maeda

Borzoi House

Photographs:
Hiroshi Shinozawa

**Katsuura Chiba,
Japan**

The highly experimental design for this house arose from two very specific requirements from the client. On one hand, she stipulated that the home should provide a sense of security, a feeling of looking inward; and on the other, she wanted to ensure that her pet dog, a borzoi, could not get out easily. Added to this was the architect's own passion for surfing, which he translated into the very layout in the form of a breaking wave.

"All is one inside a curving wave. Just as all the air for the living space within this giant metal curve is one," says Maeda. Thus, the floor plan for this single-story home is simple, punctuated only by three voids which bring ample light into the home and which have been filled with abundant vegetation, thereby avoiding a sense of confinement.

So, while Borzoi is "one air", there are paradoxes arrayed therein so that multiple sceneries unfurl simultaneously. The three gardens provide the necessary counterpoint to the spatial continuum of floor, walls and ceiling all being formed by the same curving surface. While the external view is a unified whole, the internal space displays obvious contours.

The structure is timber frame and steel, with the exterior completely sheathed in metal. Upon entering, though, the hard industrial feel instantly becomes gentle and welcoming, with the interior clad almost entirely in white gypsum plaster board.

The structure is timber frame and steel, with the exterior completely sheathed in metal. Upon entering, though, the hard industrial feel instantly becomes gentle and welcoming, with the interior clad almost entirely in white gypsum plaster board.

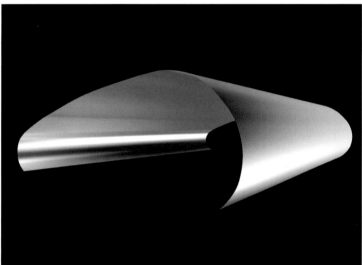

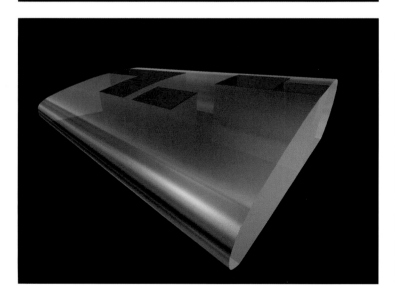

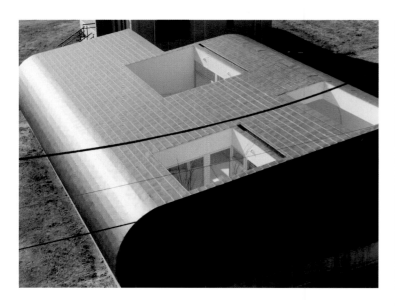

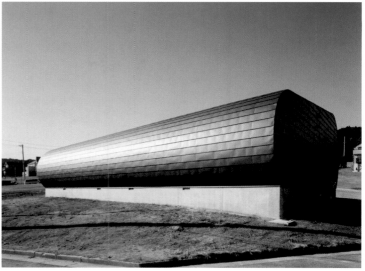

One of the guiding themes behind the design of this house was that the client's Borzoi dog should not be able to easily get out and that it should therefore have ample indoor space for exercise. The architect's response was a "runway" set along the full length of one side of the house.

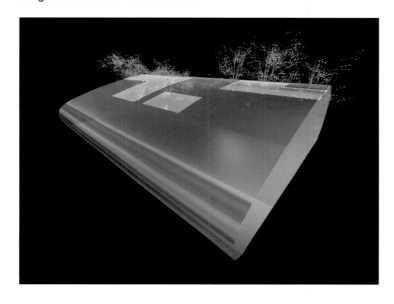

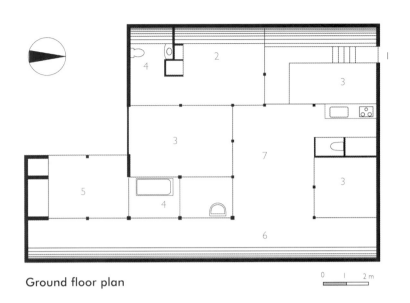

Ground floor plan

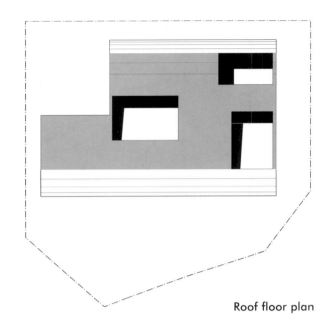

Roof floor plan

1. Entry
2. Bedroom
3. Garden
4. Bathroom

5. Tatami room
6. Dog run
7. Lounge

The structure is timber frame and steel, with the exterior completely sheathed in metal. Upon entering, though, the hard industrial feel instantly becomes gentle and welcoming, with the interior clad almost entirely in white gypsum plaster board.

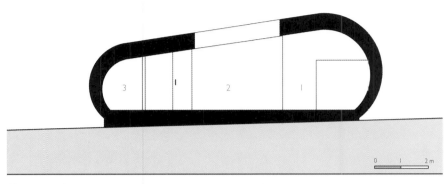

Cross section   1. Bedroom   2. Garden   3. Dog run

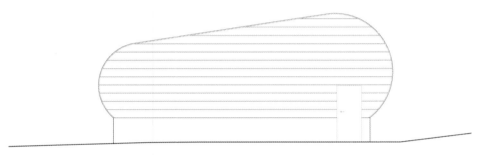

North elevation

pool Architektur

In spe-single family house

*Photographs:
Hertha Hurnaus*

Wien, Austria

The site is determined on the one hand by a slope falling gently towards the north, and on the other by two statutory regulations restricting the possible building location: it had to be adjoined to the neighboring house and was not allowed to be more than a few meters away from the street on the southern side.

One approaches the house by gentle concrete steps gradually entrenching themselves into the ground, thus leading to the sunken entrance area situated between ground and basement floor. Along with the access steps a car ramp, which, among other things, can also be used as a covered parking space or to play table tennis, runs down to the basement level.

The kitchen/dining area, open completely to the south, is a few steps above entrance level. From this three-meter-high space, four steps lead up to the somewhat lower-height living area, expanding into the garden on the north side.

A sliding door provides access to a terrace, beyond which lie a swimming pool and garden. Turning around again, the slope of the entrance hill leads to a working area situated on top of it, between ground and first floor. Here, sunlight shines into the ground floor, and one has a fair view of the landscape and home.

Another turn, and after some steps one arrives at a small room which provides access to three individual rooms, a bathroom and a small terrace on the south side. From here, a steel stairway leads up to the roof, offering a marvellous view over Lainzerbach.

Roof plan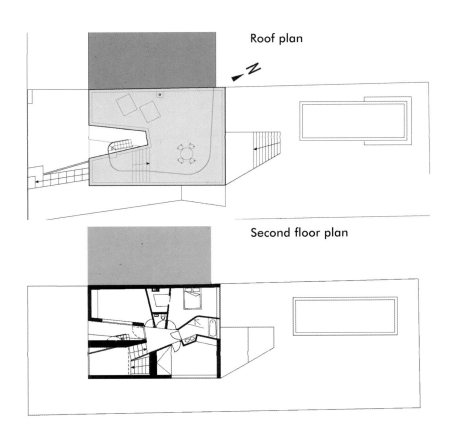

Second floor plan

First floor plan   0 1   3 m

Basement floor plan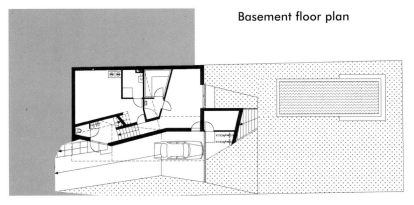

East elevation

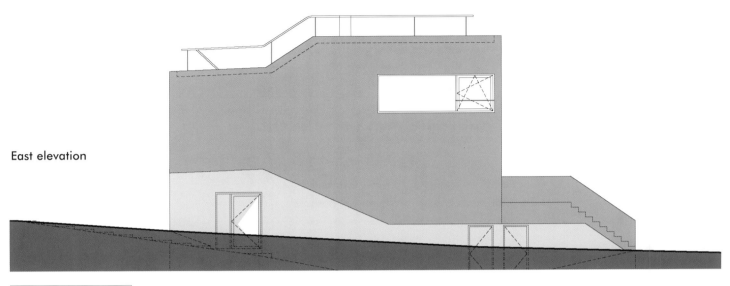

South elevation

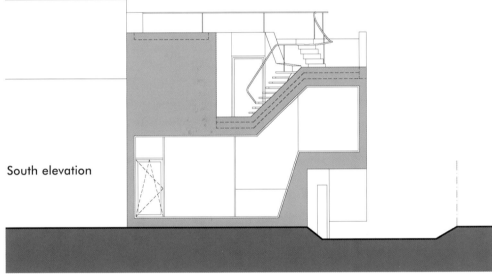

The northern and southern elevations are cut open completely, the southern glazed facade flooding the interior with light. Once inside, visitors find themselves in the inside of a cut-up hill, looking down on the one side to the basement, on the other side climbing up into the living area on the ground fllor.

Longitudinal section

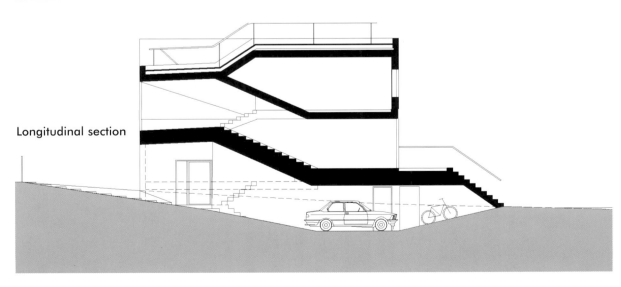

Procter:Rihl

Slice House

Photographs:
Marcelo Nunes, Sue

Porto Alegre, Brasil

The Slice House project was selected to represent Brazil in the IV Latin American Architecture Biennale in October 2004 in Peru. The house makes a series of references to modern Brazilian architecture as well as adding a new element with its complex prismatic geometry, which generates a series of spatial illusions in the interior spaces. The project is placed on a site measuring 12.14 feet in width and 126.31 feet in length (3.7 m X 38.5 m). Having been vacant for more than 20 years, it had already gone to auction 3 times without any interest whatsoever. The present client was the only one to put in an offer on the 4th auction, as the general bidders could not see the potential.

The project that was eventually decided upon for the renovation uses prismatic geometry with flush details, which demands more careful detailing and site supervision. Remodeling in 3D allowed adjustments to ensure accuracy and precision of delivered components with final sizing on site. Windows, metalwork, and cabinetwork were assembled to fit on-site. These elements were crafted precisely, in contrast to the intentionally rough concrete surfaces.

Wood-formed cast concrete was preferred since it is a local tradition, and pre-cast concrete or metal formwork is not generally available for this size of a project. The wood formwork was built in situ with a plank pattern emphasizing wood grain, accidental texture pattern, and imperfections. The ceilings were cast at a slope angle of 10 degrees, a familiar technique in the Brazilian building process. The terrace and swimming pool employ an in situ technology of resin and fiberglass coatings applied on site after the concrete cured completely.

Probably the best feature of the house is the crafted metal work. The 22.97-foot-long (7 m) kitchen counter is a continuous steel slab with 6.56-foot (2 m) cantilevered tables floating off of both ends at the dining and courtyard sides. The thick steel plate folds up transitionally between the lower dining height and higher work counter. The steel work surface is coated with avocado-colored, two-part catalyzed laboratory paint providing an extremely hard finish. The stair features a .31 inch (8 mm) steel plate accordion folded and welded in sections onto the undercarriage beam plates. Because the stair is a "U" shape with offset forces, the engineers were able to design thinner and lighter balustrade details than normal.

Wood-formed cast concrete was preferred since it is a local tradition, and pre-cast concrete or metal formwork is not generally available for this size of a project. The wood formwork was built in situ with a plank pattern emphasizing wood grain, accidental texture pattern, and imperfections.

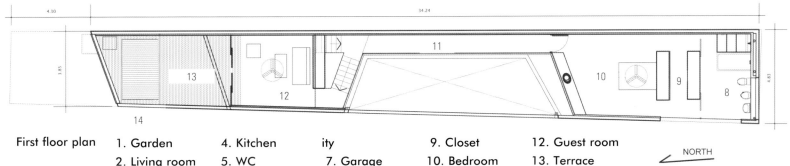

First floor plan

1. Garden	4. Kitchen	ity	9. Closet	12. Guest room
2. Living room	5. WC	7. Garage	10. Bedroom	13. Terrace
3. Dining room	6. Garage util-	8. Bathroom	11. Hall	14. Pool

NORTH

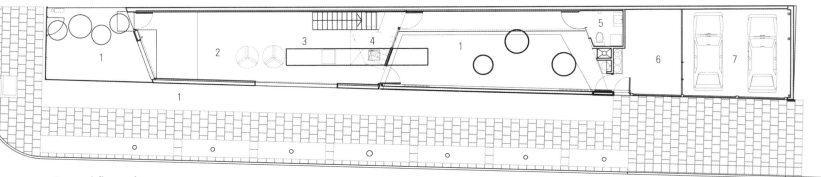

Ground floor plan

© Marcelo Nunes

The ceilings were cast at a slope angle of 10 degrees, a familiar technique in the Brazilian building process. The terrace and swimming pool employ an in situ technology of resin and fiberglass coatings applied on site after the concrete cured completely.

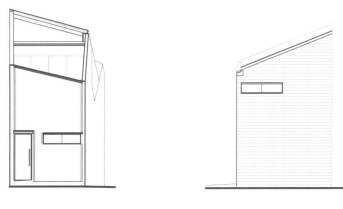

North elelvation   South elelvation

© Marcelo Nunes

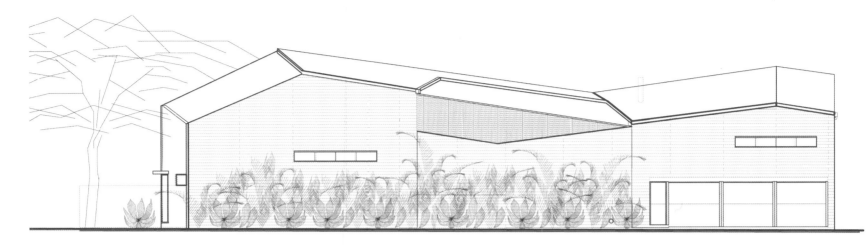

West elelvation WEST ELEVATION

© Marcelo Nunes

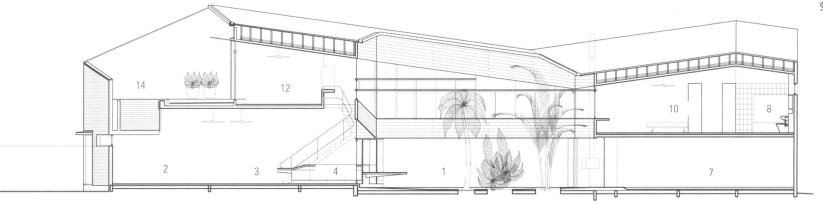

Longitudinal section

1. Garden	4. Kitchen	7. Garage	10. Bedroom	13. Terrace
2. Living room	5. WC	8. Bathroom	11. Hall	14. Pool
3. Dining room	6. Garage utility	9. Closet	12. Guest room	

Propeller Z

DBL House

Photographs: Margherita Spliuttini

Vienna, Austria

Located on the western outskirts of Vienna, the site of DBL House measures roughly 5382 sq ft (500 sqm), with an allowable footprint limited to 947 sq ft (88 sqm) by building bylaws. The program called for two individual units of approximately 1076 sq ft (100 sqm) each, forcing the structure to expand to the very limits of the maximum volume made possible by the building code.

The allocation of space between the two units, which are occupied by two sisters, was developed in a process in which both occupants were given the possibility to choose from a variety of parameters, such as orientation, lighting, access to the garden, privacy, transparency etc. The evaluation of this process resulted in two markedly different profiles for the units. The slightly smaller one was to be rather closed, but with connection to the south facing street, the larger one was to be transparent and open, with direct access to the garden.

Unit one is organized as a compact volume, the main areas being connected by split-level circulation with a ramp connecting the topmost sleeping box with the lower areas. The whole unit is constructed as a rigid concrete box, which, as a whole is raised above the ground, resting only on the concrete staircase and on three thin steel struts. It thus liberates the ground, forming a roof under which the second unit is located.

With all the necessary structure provided by the first unit, the second is an open space, which is enclosed with glass or light marine plywood walls with a glass strip separating the two units along the whole perimeter. The interior flooring in both units is a combination of hardwood parquet and epoxy resin.

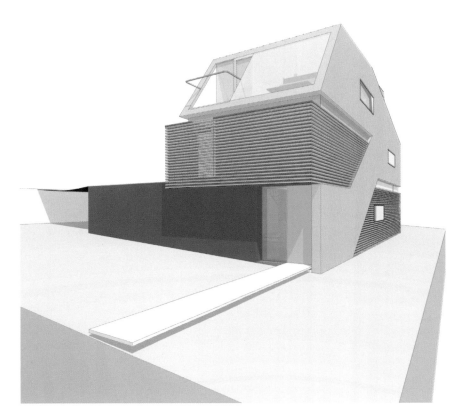

Unit one is organized as a compact volume, the main areas being connected by split-level circulation with a ramp connecting the topmost sleeping box with the lower areas. With all the necessary structure provided by the first unit, the second is an open space, which is enclosed with glass.

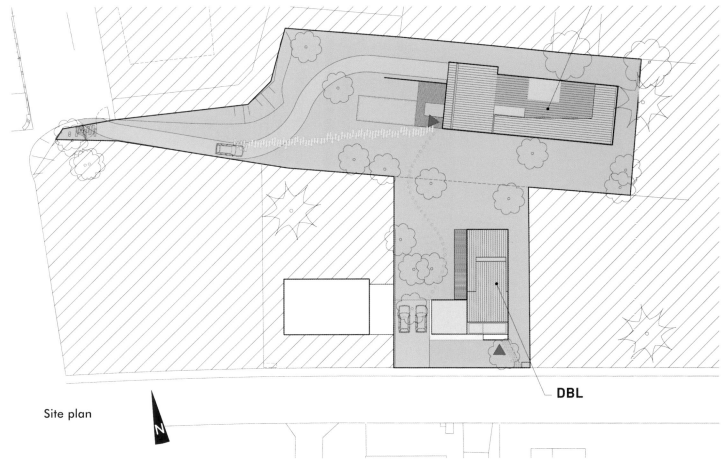

DBL

Site plan

N

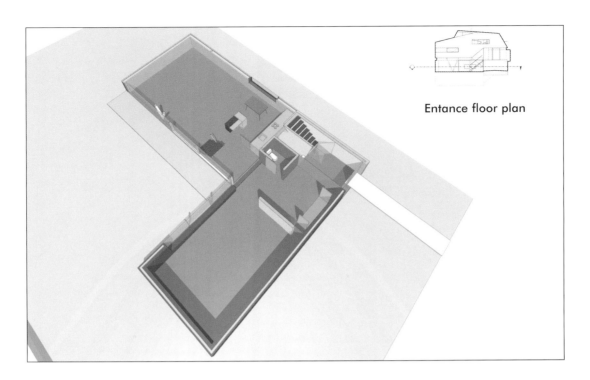

Entance floor plan

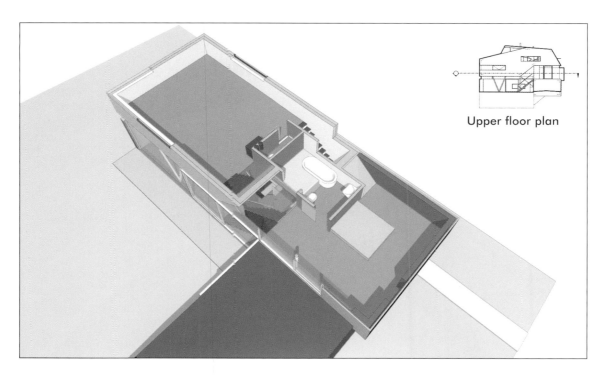

Upper floor plan

Tom Maine-Morphosis

Blades Residence

Photographs: kim zwarts

Santa Barbara, USA

In June 1990 several hundred homes in the coastal hills of Santa Barbara were destroyed by fire. The clients decided to reframe this catastrophic experience as a catalyst to reinvent their day-to-day existence. Unlike their neighbors who took more "conventional" approaches, they decided to build a house "like nothing they had ever seen before".

The fire left a charred landscape with a gentle sloping grade, several boulders and a cluster of native oaks. Given its suburban/rural context, the introspective strategy for an enclosed project was explored.

Due to the very modest budget, design and craftsmanship were given priority over expensive materials from the very first moment.

The 3800 feet of interior ground area is organized as three main spaces adjacent to five smaller exterior rooms, each one a linear sequence of overlapping zones in which the boundaries of public and private spaces are intentionally blurred. Interior light is modulated through subtle openings and recesses that create a sculpted space. The couple shares a very open bedroom, yet each has their individual studios at opposite ends of the house. The upper story studio has expansive views from a corner window that has been carved out as well as an exterior catwalk. The ground floor studio/gallery is a separate wing with clerestory windows and no exterior views.

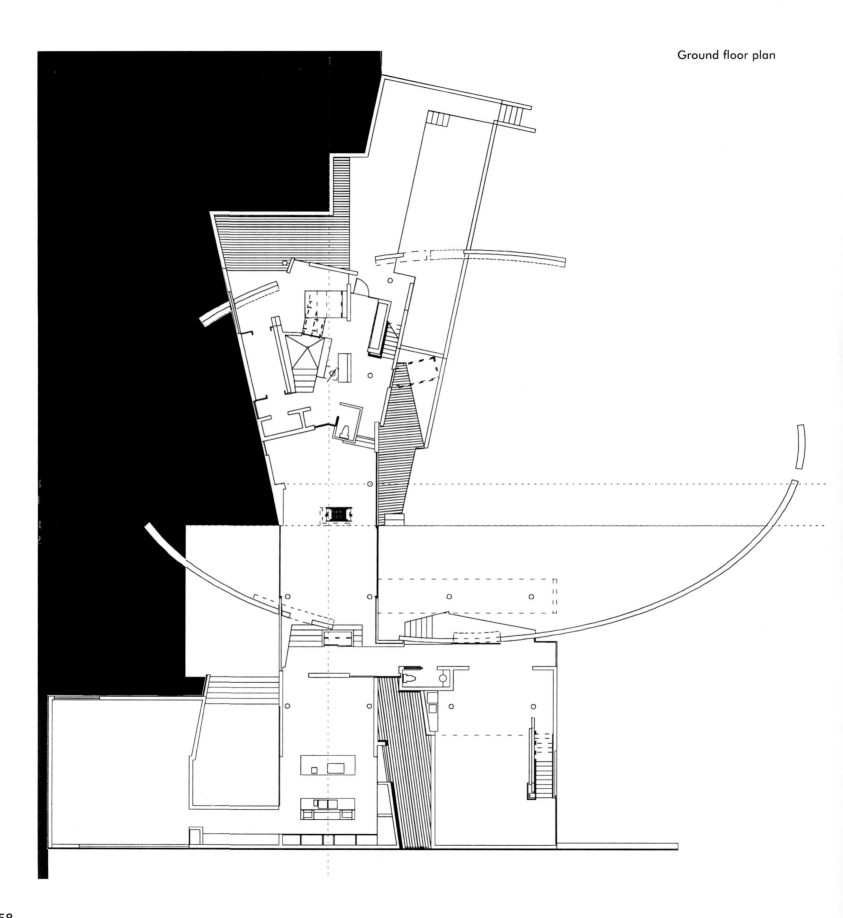

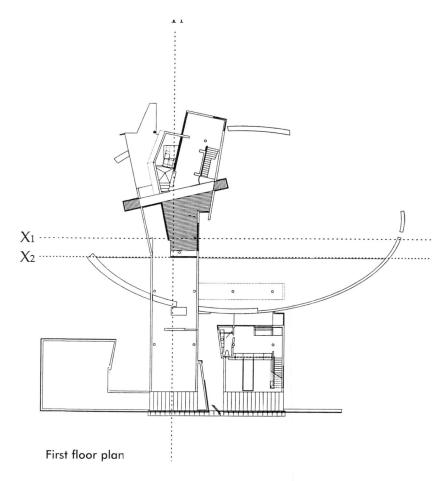

X_1
X_2

First floor plan

The interior of the dwelling is organized as a large single space that is almost entirely uninterrupted.

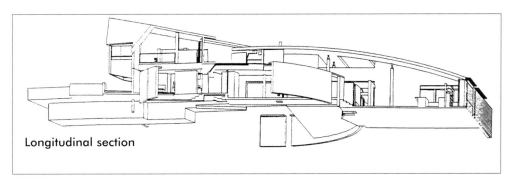

Longitudinal section

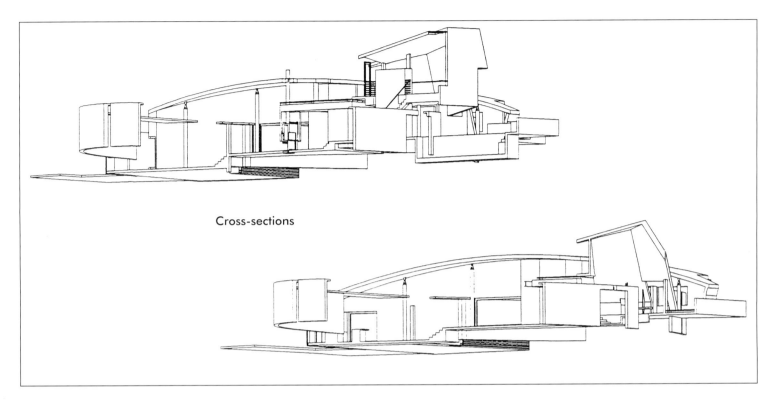

Cross-sections

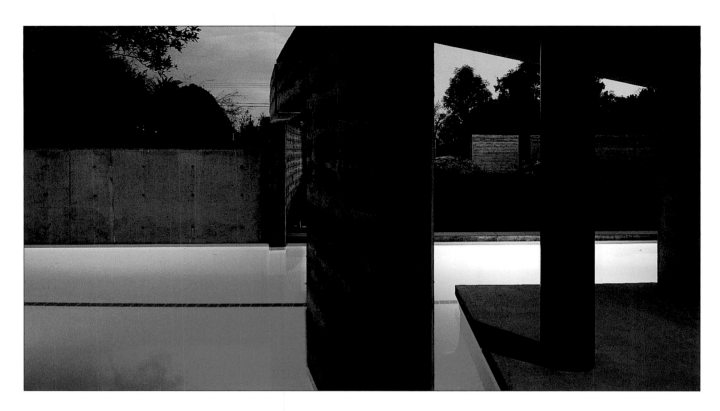

Un Studio Van Berkel & Bos

Möbius House

Photographs: Christian Richters

**Het Gooi,
The Netherlands**

The diagram of the double-locked torus conveys the organization of two intertwining paths, which trace how two people can live together, yet apart, meeting at certain points, which become shared spaces. The idea of two entities running their own trajectories but sharing certain moments, possibly also reversing roles at certain points, is extended to include the materialization of the building and its construction.

The Möbius house integrates program, circulation and structure seamlessly. The house interweaves the various states that accompany the condensation of differentiating activities into one structure: work, social life, family life and individual time alone all find their places in the loop structure. Movement through this loop follows the pattern of an active day. The structure of movement is transposed to the organization of the two main materials used for the house; glass and concrete move in front of each other and switch places. Concrete construction becomes furniture and glass facades turn into inside partition walls.

As a graphic representation of 24 hours of family life, the diagram acquires a time-space dimension, which leads to the implementation of the Möbius band. Equally the site and its relationship to the building are important for the design. The site covers two hectares, which are divided into four distinct areas. Linking these with the internal organization of the Möbius band transforms living in the house into a walk in the landscape.

The mathematical model of the Möbius is not literally transferred to the building, but is conceptualized and can be found in architectural ingredients, such as the light, the staircases and the way in which people move through the house. So, while the Möbius diagram introduces aspects of duration and trajectory, the diagram is worked into the building in a mutated way.

The instrumentalization of this simple drawing is the key. The two interlocking lines are suggestive of the formal organization of the building, but that is only the beginning; diagrammatic architecture is a process of unfolding and ultimately of liberation. The diagram liberates architecture from language, interpretation and signification.

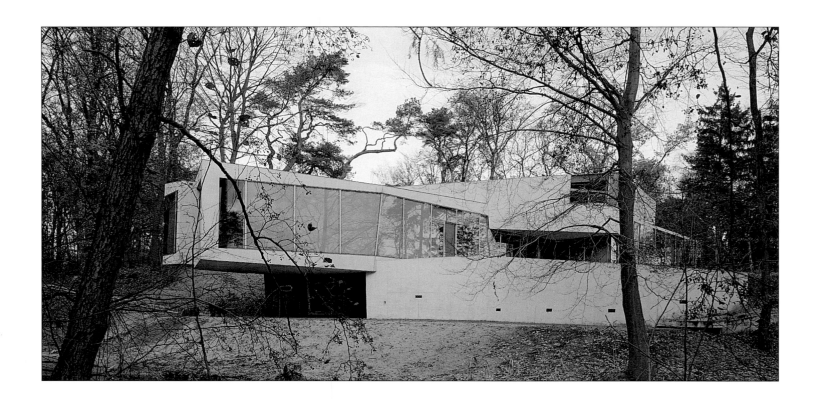

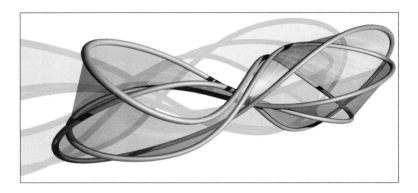

Bedroom

Studio 01

Circulation
Bathroom

Toilet
Ramp
Garage

Storage

Meeting room

Circulation
Kitchen

Verandah

Living room

Fireplace

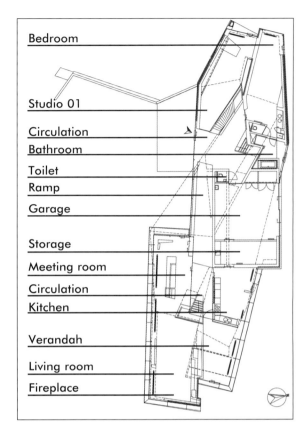

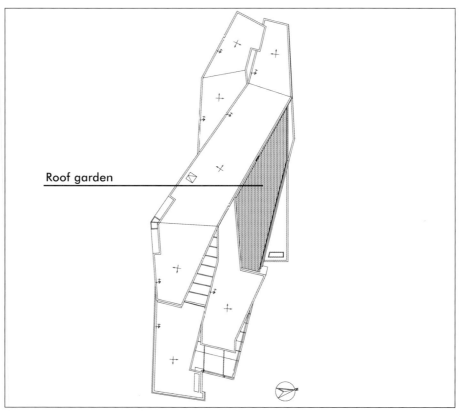

Roof garden

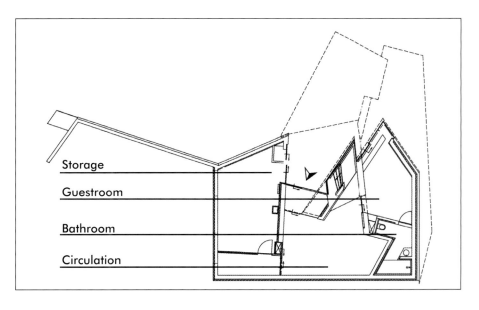

Storage

Guestroom

Bathroom

Circulation

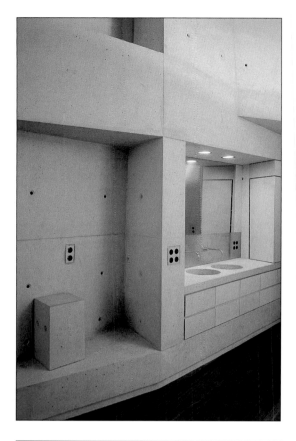

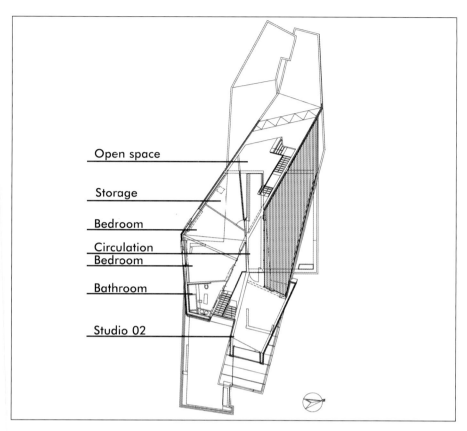

Open space

Storage

Bedroom

Circulation
Bedroom

Bathroom

Studio 02

Ushida Findlay Partnership

Polyphony

Photographs: Katsuhisa Kida,
Takeshi Taira

Osaka, Japan

Located on a site in a suburb of Osaka created for the Exhibition of 1970, this original dwelling was conceived for a couple of musicians and their children. Music and architecture seem to converge in this building, which bears a certain resemblance to the structure of the inner ear.

Polyphony is a musical term that refers to the overlapping of sounds in a composition. Authors like Bartok, who incorporated popular songs in his works, and John Cage, who introduced the sound created by the public and the space, paved the way for contemporary music, which uses sampling and mixes to create sound atmospheres full of superimposed nuances.

The combination of sound and construction has a long tradition in Japan, where materials and vegetation (such as bamboo to transform the wind into music and attract birds) are often chosen for the acoustic effect that they give. In the design of this dwelling, conceived so that its inhabitants could experience the sounds of the environment as part of a total sensorial experience, the aim was to create a space that had a correlation with the repetitive acoustic cycles.

The ground plan of the dwelling is based on a geometric pattern on which circles of 3.4 m in diameter are traced around a main circle, achieving an original form similar to that of a slightly curved sausage. This winding tube is cut diagonally, so that the solid is gradually transformed into a void. The overlapping of cylinders to generate a space of multiple layers is directly related to the effect of the chords formed by superimposed sounds.

In accordance with the visual experience of the space, it was intended to create a sound landscape in which it was possible to experience a range of unexpected acoustic effects. This was achieved by means of curved walls forming a series of corridors that seem to whisper and give off strange echoes as if one held a shell to one's ear. These curved forms are repeated in the whole house and make the interior an enveloping place full of winding corners in which the furniture and the openings play a major role.

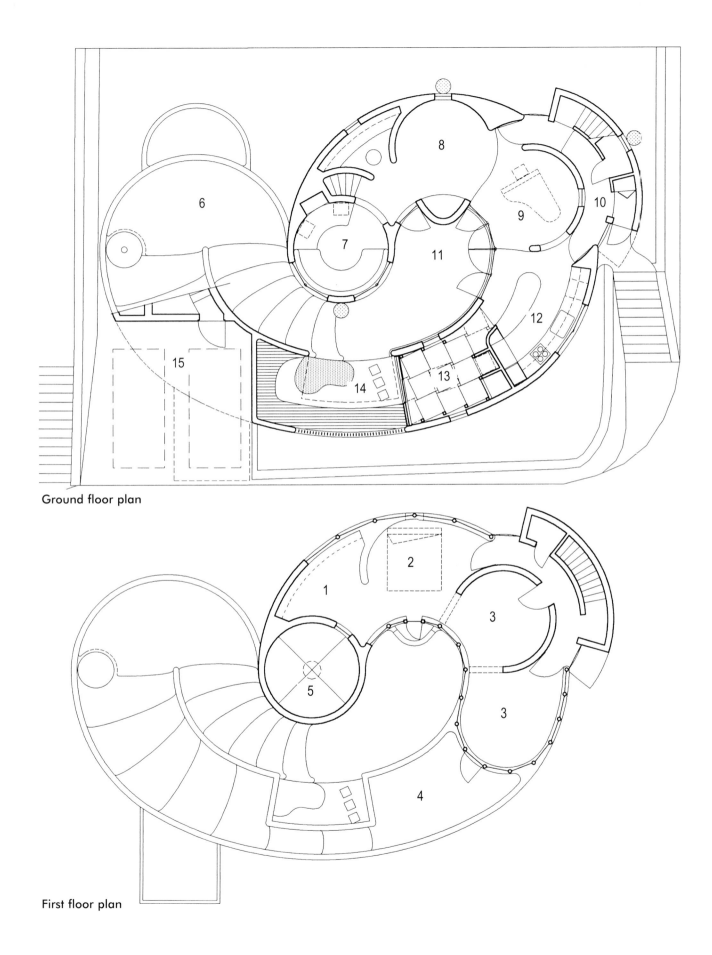

Ground floor plan

First floor plan

The ground plan of the dwelling is based on a geometric pattern on which circles of 3.4 m diameter are traced around a main circle. This creates a winding, tubular space that appears to be cut diagonally so that the solid is gradually transformed into a void.

1. Wardrobe
2. Main bedroom
3. Bedroom
4. Terrace
5. Void
6. Kids patio
7. Audio zone
8. Family zone
9. Piano zone
10. Entrance
11. Courtyard
12. Kitchen-dining
13. Japanese room
14. Garden
15. Garage
16. Bathroom

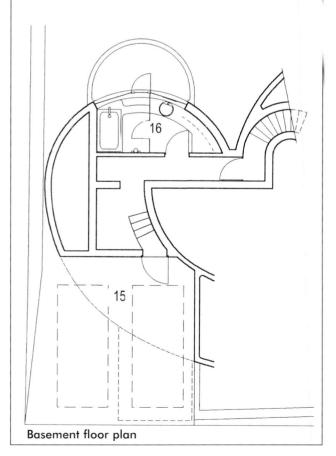

Basement floor plan

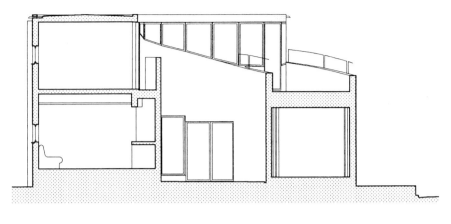

The curved walls were intended to create a landscape in which the inhabitants could experience the sounds of the environment as part of a total sensorial experience.

North-south section

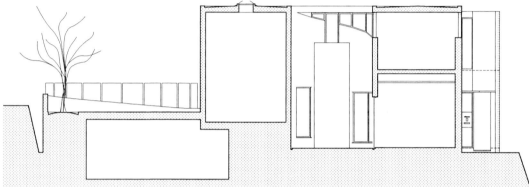

East-west section

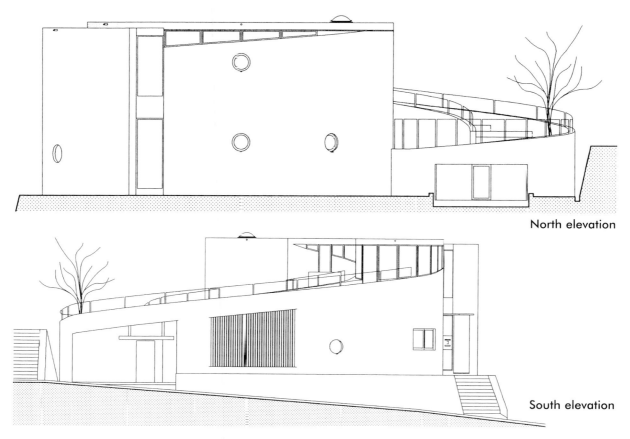

North elevation

South elevation

Querkraft

Dra Single Family Dwelling

Photographs: Querkraft

Vienna, Austria

This project posed a dilemma for the architects. The site was a perfect sunny slope with a panoramic view of the city of Vienna, but it was also quite small, and the usable building area even smaller: what to do with such large views and such a small space? The problem was resolved by stacking, a solution which created the ideal situation of large views and lots of space.

The floor area is spread over two stories, but the entire structure is elevated over the garden. Only a third of the building is attached to the ground on a base of reinforced concrete, with the remaining two thirds protecting a space in the garden that can be used as another living space in the summertime. There are four levels in total, the reclaimed garden area, the entry level with a spiral staircase leading up to the third floor containing the cooking, dining and living areas and views over the city, and the roof. The terrace compensates for the "lost" area on the ground in order to maximize the use of space in such a small site.

In order to support the enormous projection out from the base and the open plan interior, the structure is made of steel. Three principal two-storey steel frames carry the load, with the two side frames jutting out 6 meters to support the main, 15-meter long structure. It supports several beams that lead into the center of the building, completing the construction.

The living spaces are installed on one side of this steel structure, while the terraces are on the other. The two are unified rather than separated by a glass membrane, which is penetrated by several steel roof beams. The effect is of spatial unity, and the eye can range through the space with no structural elements hindering the panoramic view.

The architecture does not make a distinction between rooms and terraces, with a polygonal geometry of lines that increases the independence of each element. Inclined angles break the rectangular forms and give them a certain formal stability, intensified by the windows placed around the corners of the building.

West elevation

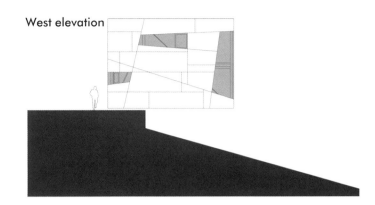

North elevation

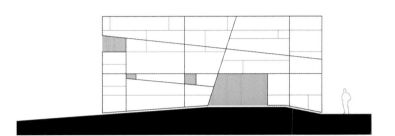

East elevation

South elevation

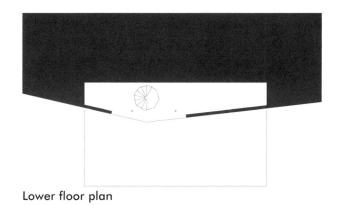

Lower floor plan

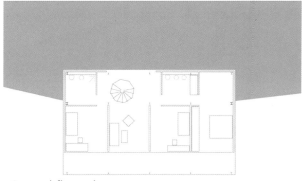

Ground floor plan

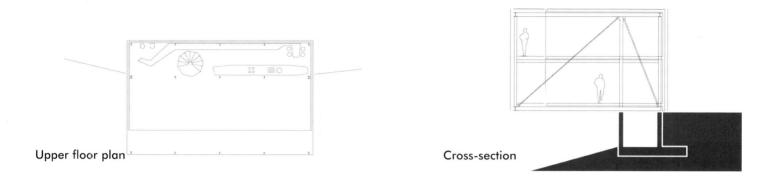

Upper floor plan   Cross-section

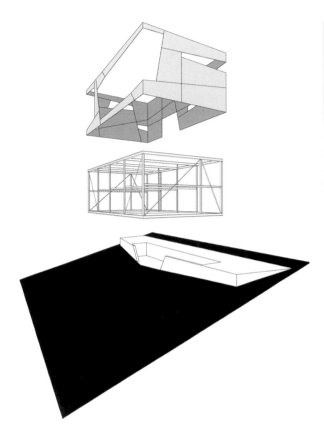

Querkraft

SPS one-family detached house

Photographs: Querkraft

Vienna, Austria

This house is situated on a quiet piece of land with panoramic views over Vienna, orientated towards the southeast. The position in an allotment settlement area (the construction area of max. 50 square meters per building unit) had to be newly and favorably interpreted for a house with an effective area of nearly 300 square meters to be created.

The main building was set into the hillside, as far in the rear of the property as possible to position an optimally large garden area in front of the building. House and garden represent a confluent living unit for over two thirds of the year. The transition from indoors to the outdoor garden is accentuated by a shading device constructed as a scaffolding in a deep terrace area.

Constructing the living spaces dug into the hillside in the form of a cellar made it possible according to the building code to have 83 instead of 50 square meters surface.

The parental bedroom and a second "special" living room have been added on top of the hillside house. The breathtaking panoramic views can be enjoyed daily by the owners on waking up and falling asleep. This floor has been designed in order to have the maximum view without obstructing at the same time the views of the surrounding houses.

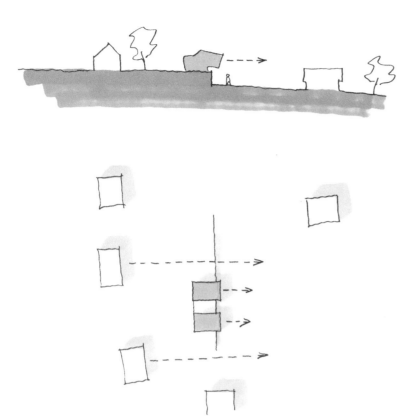

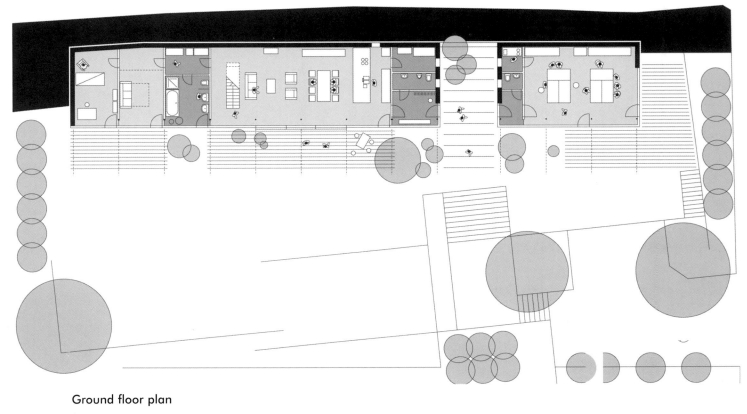

Ground floor plan

0 l   5 m

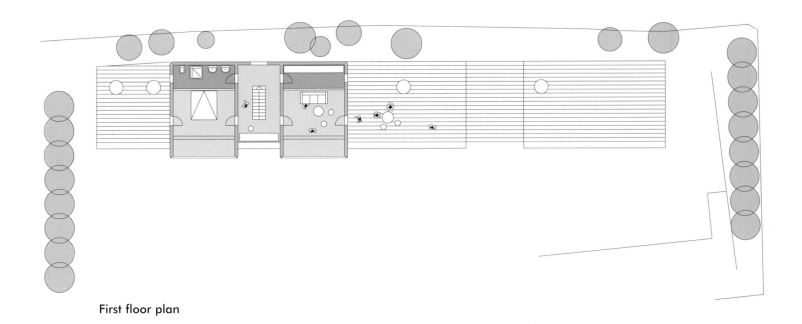

First floor plan

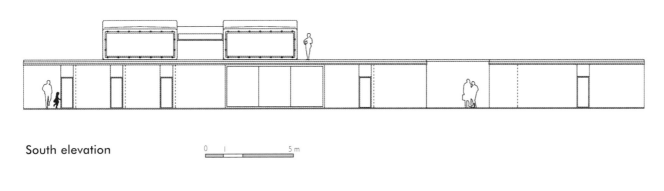

South elevation

0 | 5 m

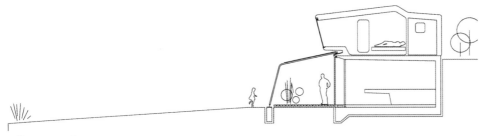

Cross section

The house is designed so that the gorgeous views crown and penetrate everyday life without dominating it.

Atelier Tekuto

Cell Brick House

Photographs: Makoto Yoshida

Tokyo, Japan

Cell Brick House sits on the corner lot of a tranquil Tokyo residential area. Tokyo based architect Yasuhiro Yamashita constructed the building, and the skin layering helps create a unique dwelling that applies a new form of masonry. He calls this form of construction "void masonry". The boxes do not serve just to make structure, but also become storage units in the house's interior. They also work to create a brise-soleil light control, allowing the building to respond to the heat of the environment.

The steel boxes used here measure 900 x 450 x 300 mm, and the thickness of the portion facing outside stands at 9 mm. By piling them up in units rather than individually they succeeded in creating a modern design. Since the assembled box units do not fit together perfectly, light is brought into the interior at periodic intervals.

Among the several novel ideas that the client proposed for the project, one example is the bathroom, which is situated so as to appear to be floating; another such idea incorporated into the design was the washing machine sitting on the way up a spiral staircase.

The building takes up three levels from the first floor basement to the above ground second floor. The ground area encompasses 32.93 sqm with a total built area of 85.05 sqm, and a height of 6.685 meters. In the next project, they constructed the structure of glass blocks, semi-translucent blocks and transparent blocks, instead of steel boxes.

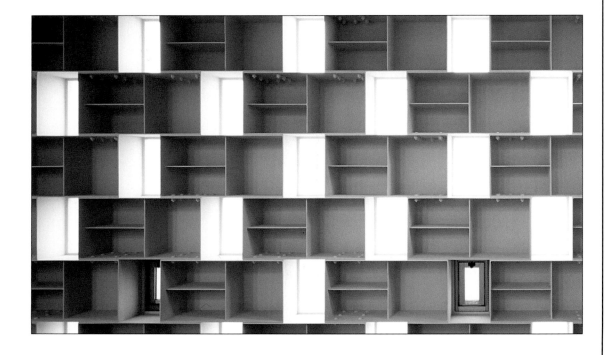

199

At first glance, the Cell Brick House seems to be a structure of piled-up concrete blocks, but on closer inspection one sees that these blocks are in fact steel boxes.

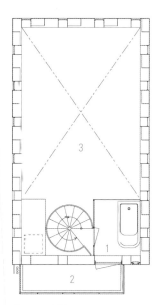

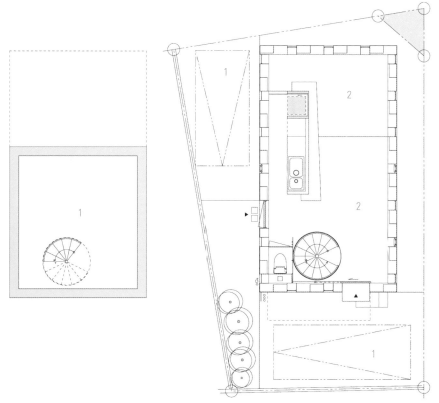

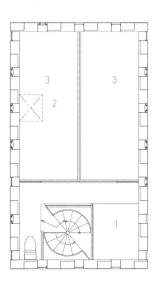

Ground Floor

1. Room 1

First Floor

1. Car

2. Dining-living room

3. Bedroom

Second Floor

1. Bathroom

2. Terrace

3. Void

Third Floor

1. Loft

2. Top light

3. Bedroom

Interior elevation

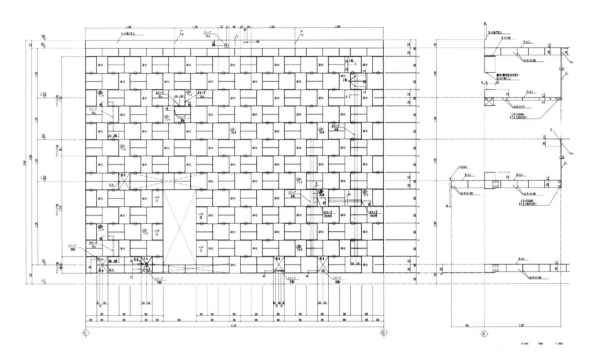

Model analysis

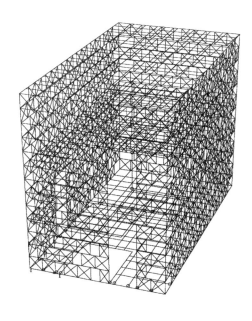

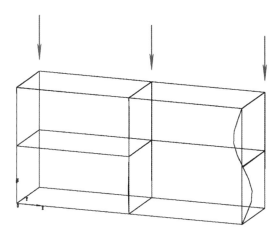

The house is for a family of three: a single parent and two children. The facade's composition of alternating steel blocks and voids is seen in the interior as a succession of storage spaces broken up by dozens of windows that bring abundant natural light into the home.

RCR arquitectes
Aranda, Pigem, Vilalta

M-Lidia House

Photographs: Eugeni Pons

This house was built on a simple, straightforward site with good views. It was designed with a limited budget for a young couple without children.

The building consists of a metallic box structure with thin walls and glass protected by metallic mesh that opens the space towards the exterior, creating gaps that are perfect for managing the wind.

A concrete slab was used for the foundation, and a steel frame for the metallic structure. The metallic box was assembled in the workshop, and rests on walls that form an enclosed, partly underground area that contains the garage.

In section, with all the services grouped together, the interior space is defined by the thin or the thick walls. The space can be divided in three or left open, depending on the placement of the glass walls in the gaps. These change the perception of space in relation to its size, relative emptiness or fullness and its exterior-interior qualities.

Montagut, Girona, Spain

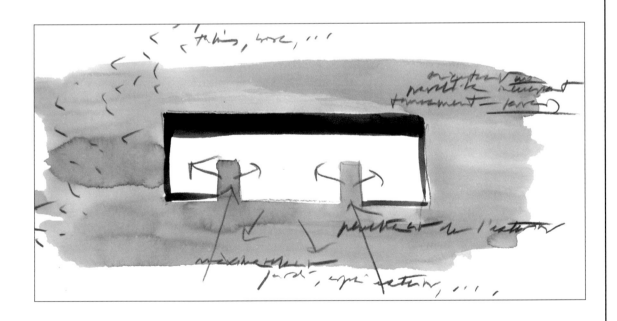

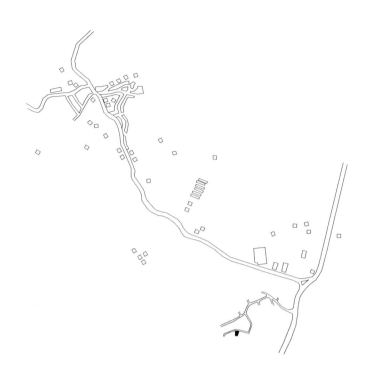

Site plan

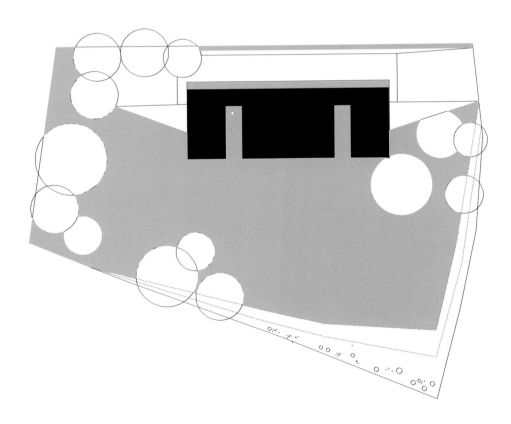

First floor

Front elevation

Section AA

Section BB

Section CC

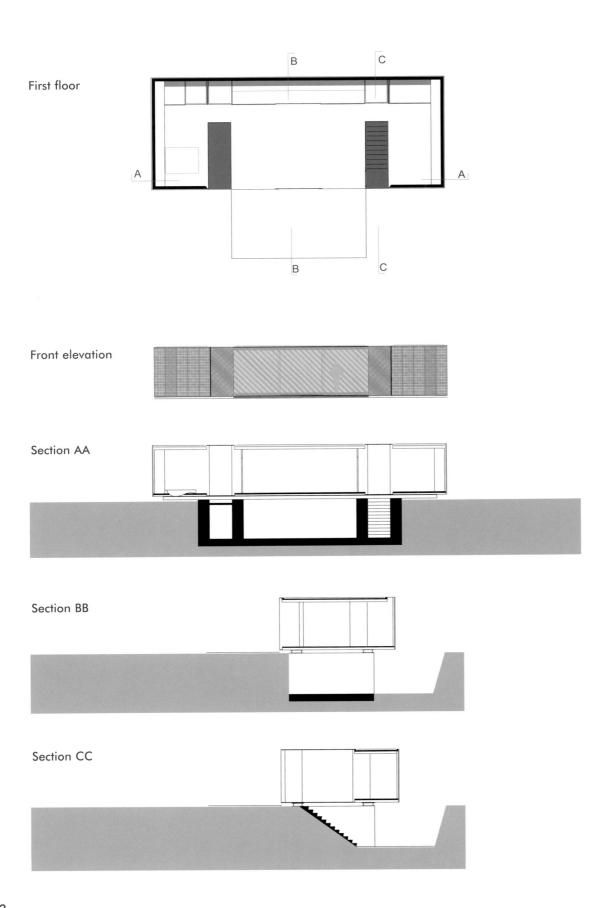

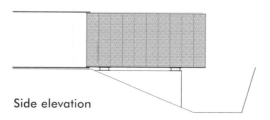

Side elevation

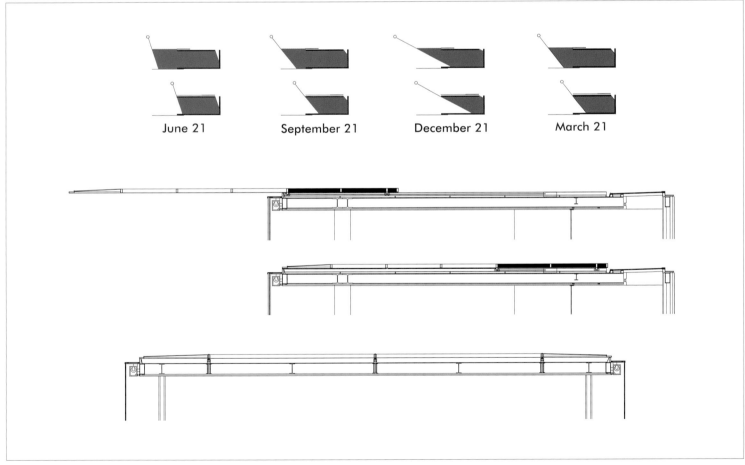

June 21   September 21   December 21   March 21

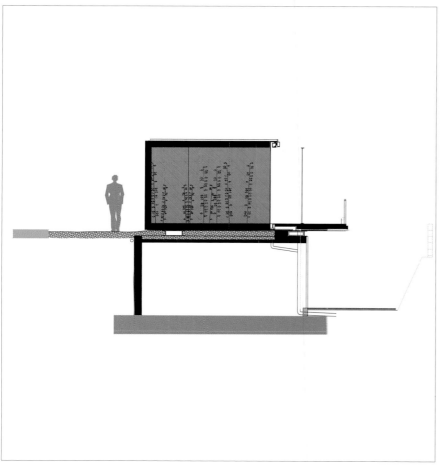

Aldo Celoria

Travella House

Photographs: Milo Keller

Castel San Pietro, Ticino, Switzerland

The site for this house, with its 351 square meters of usable surface area, is set on the gentle slope of a low hill in Castel San Pietro. This low residential zone is characterized by the presence of terraced vineyards facing the landscape.

The basis for the design was the idea of fluidity, both inside and out, starting with connecting the access road to the vineyards.

All of the infrastructure necessary for living is condensed along a transversal strip. This topography even spans the domestic spaces: the road and parking area, the stairs, the edge of the water, views from the terrace, the living room, the slope of the hill and the border of the vineyard. All the spaces are interconnected, communicating with each other in a dynamic sequence of solids and voids.

The interior spaces flow from narrowness to expansion, always creating different relations within the overall context. The structure and distribution are defined by a continuous concrete wall, which integrates the primary functions and furnishings of the house. Its thickness varies to create a volumetric and plastic interplay in a constant state of flux, from the bookshelves to the stairs, from the fireplace to the kitchen and finally becoming the outermost wall on the terraced roof.

On the second floor, where the bedrooms are, natural light is provided by a constellation of windows that determines very specific views toward the landscape.

The facade is composed of two complementary parts. Continuous glazing wraps around the perimeter of the ground floor, providing very pure and direct views. The upper floor, in contrast, has been fragmented into a cladding of copper pieces that reflect the sunlight in ever-changing shades. Over time, each piece will oxidize differently, creating a vibrant surface that will change with the years.

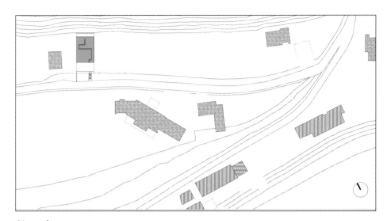

Site plan

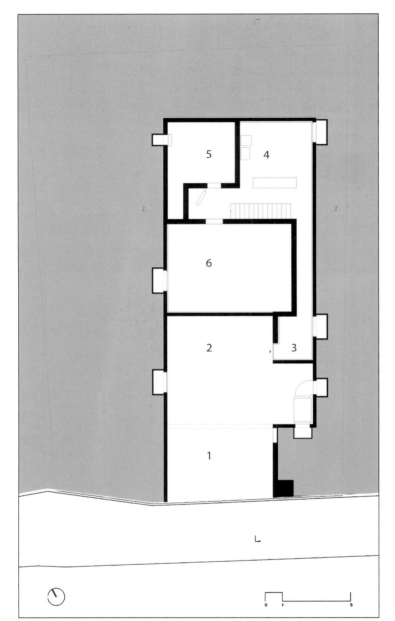

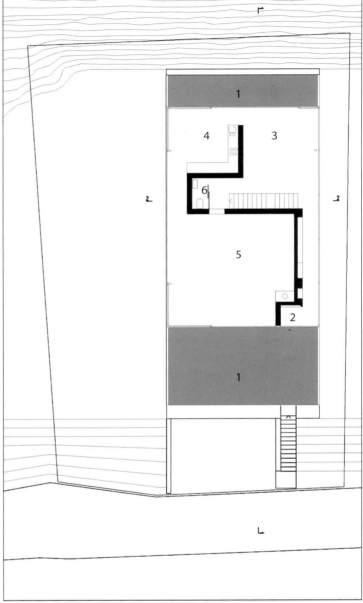

Basement plan

1. Car access
2. Garage
3. Entrance
4. Laundry
5. Atomic shelter
6. Multipurpose room

Ground floor plan

1. Terrace
2. Entrance
3. Dining
4. Kitchen
5. Living
6. Bath

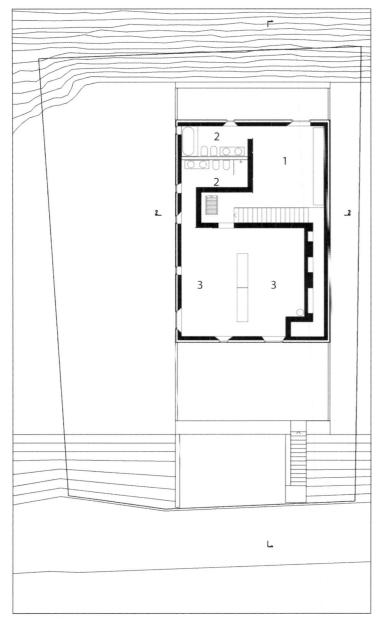

First floor plan

1. Main bedroom
2. Bath
3. Children bedroom

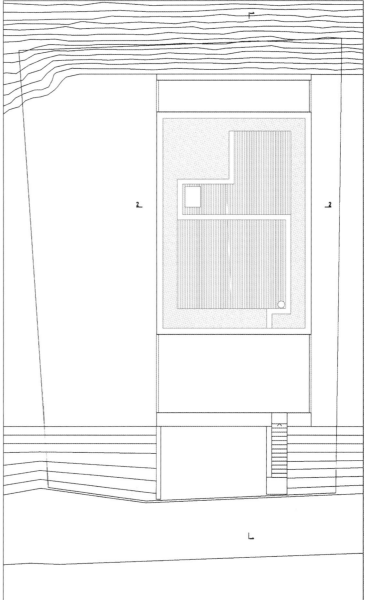

Roof plan

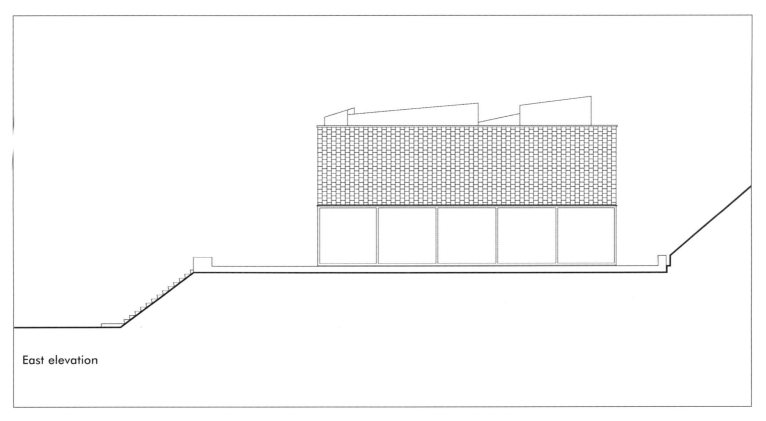

East elevation

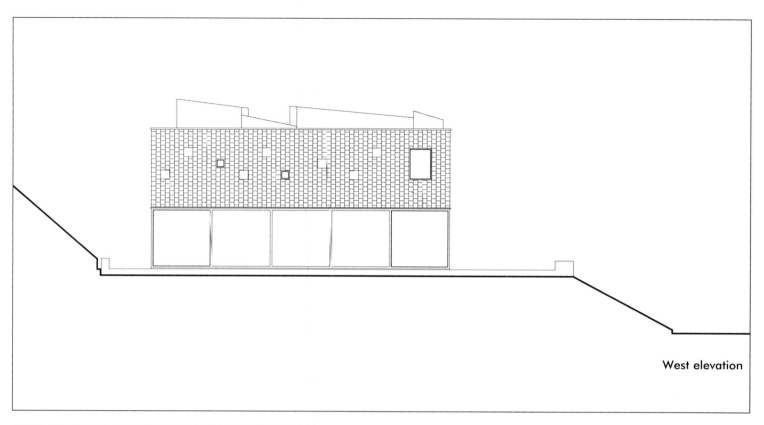

West elevation

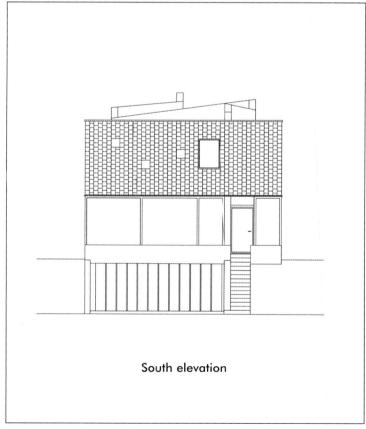

South elevation

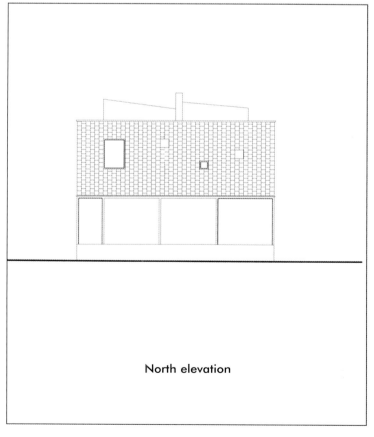

North elevation

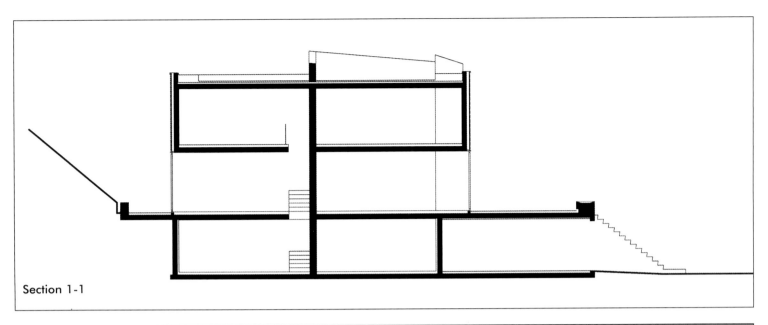

Section 1-1

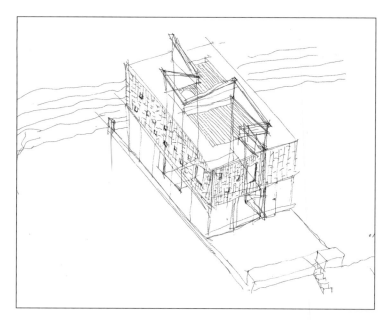

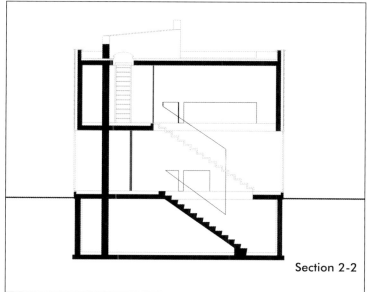

Section 2-2

Atelier Bow-Wow

Izu House

Photographs: Takashi Homma

Shizuoka, Nishizu, Japan

The client wished to completely pull up stakes from his house in Tokyo and live at a more leisurely pace in a peaceful rural setting. Arriving at the chosen site, one leaves the main road and takes a narrow path through a former tangerine plantation, the view suddenly opening outward to the immensity of Suruga Bay 100 meters below. The site is abutted on one side by a sheer cliff, giving the impression of being almost in the sky and sea. This sensation is heightened by a pier structure protruding out over the cliff.

The preliminary architectural study focused on how to implant the dwelling on such a steep incline, while also bringing the adjacent tiered field into the design scheme. At the same time, the client insisted that he did not want a home nestled too snugly into the landscape, preferring instead to challenge his corporal senses and arouse a feeling of being headed for the future. The final plan consists of a gravity-defying pier as well as a firm psychological connection to terra firma via the garden.

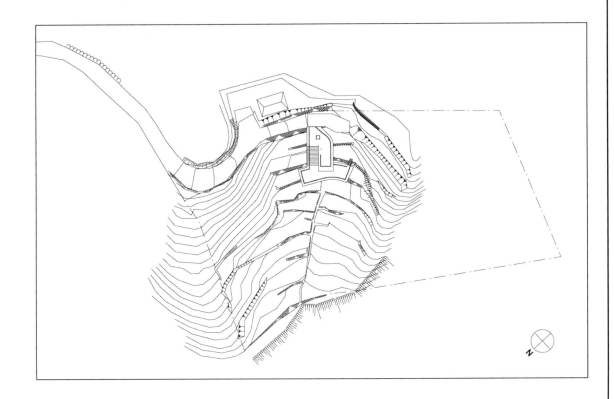

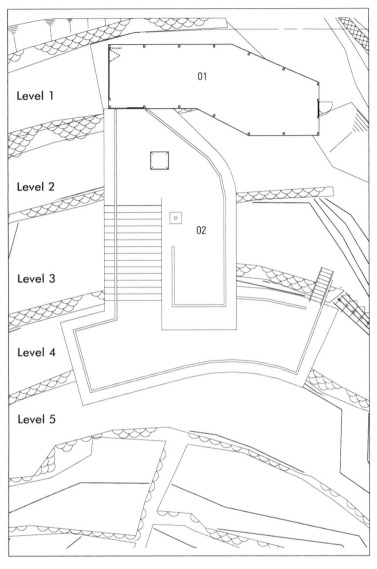

Level 1

Level 2

Level 3

Level 4

Level 5

01

02

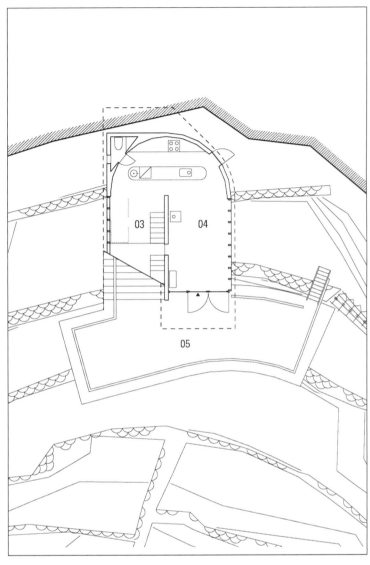

03   04

05

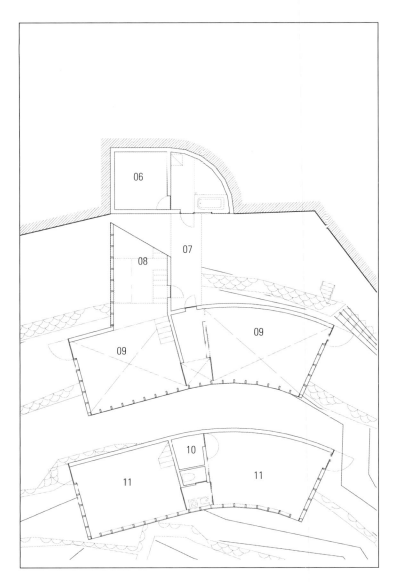

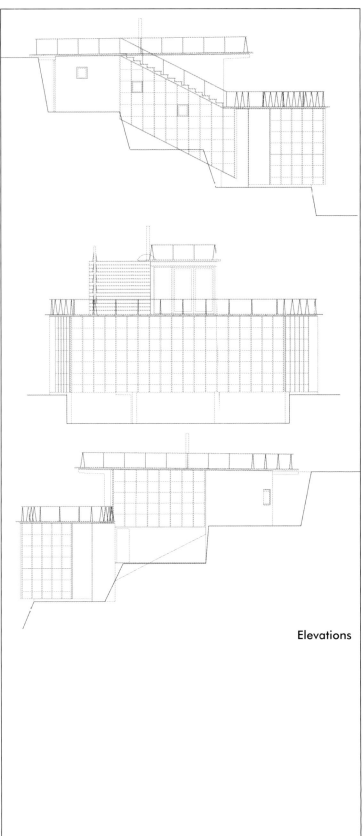

Elevations

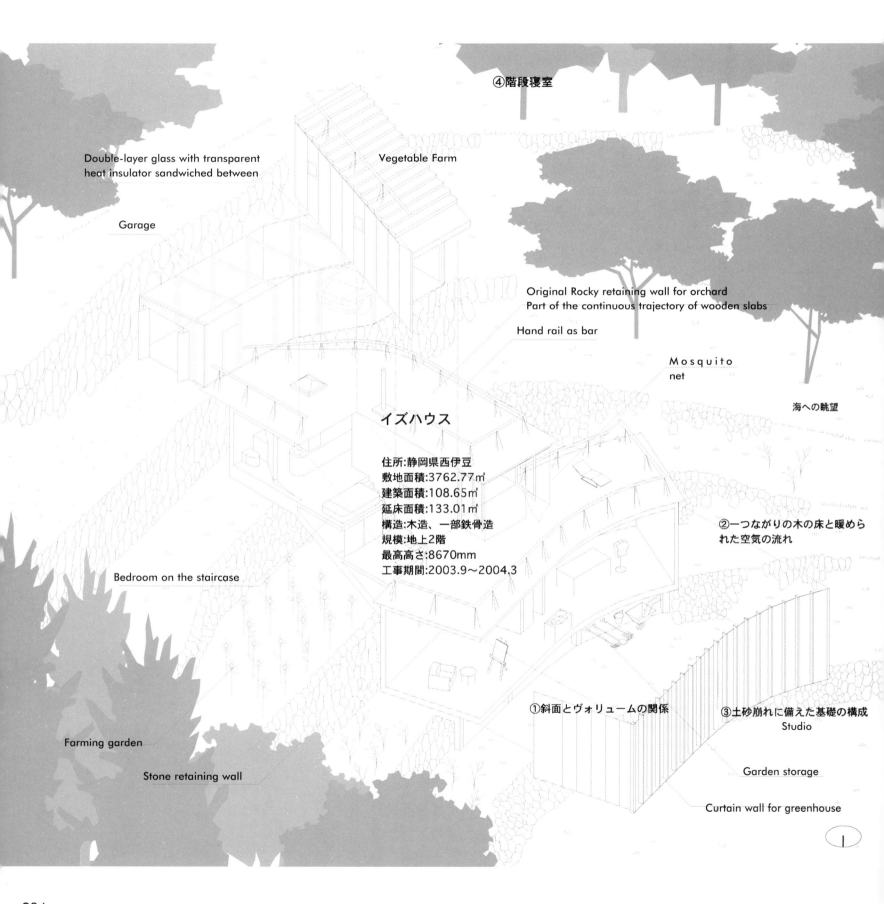

④階段寝室

Double-layer glass with transparent
heat insulator sandwiched between

Vegetable Farm

Garage

Original Rocky retaining wall for orchard
Part of the continuous trajectory of wooden slabs

Hand rail as bar

Mosquito
net

海への眺望

イズハウス

住所:静岡県西伊豆
敷地面積:3762.77㎡
建築面積:108.65㎡
延床面積:133.01㎡
構造:木造、一部鉄骨造
規模:地上2階
最高高さ:8670mm
工事期間:2003.9〜2004.3

②一つながりの木の床と暖めら
れた空気の流れ

Bedroom on the staircase

①斜面とヴォリュームの関係

③土砂崩れに備えた基礎の構成
Studio

Farming garden

Garden storage

Stone retaining wall

Curtain wall for greenhouse

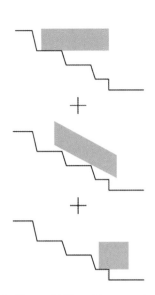

+

+

1. Slope of hill and house volume

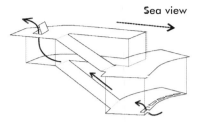

Sea view

2. Air flows along the continuous wooden slabs

3. Foundation is designed to withstand landslides

4. The stepped bedroom follows the slope of the hill, whereas the living room stretches towards the sea

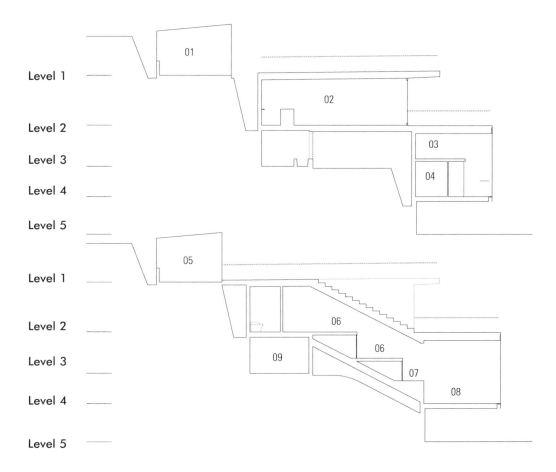

Level 1
Level 2
Level 3
Level 4
Level 5

Level 1
Level 2
Level 3
Level 4
Level 5

Sections

01. Garage
02. Living
03. Study
04. Closet
05. Garage
06. Bedroom
07. Study
08. Atelier
09. Closet